MIXED MESSAGES

Reta,
Thanks for all your
help at W.C.F.

Tod Penzig

MIXED MESSAGES

by

FRED & ANITA
PRINZING

MOODY PRESS
CHICAGO

ISBN: 0-8024-5245-0

1 2 3 4 5 6 7 8 Printing/LC/Year 96 95 94 93 92 91

To our children and their spouses,
who have demonstrated
that the message of love
can overcome the mixed messages
of the church and society

Contents

Preface   9

Acknowledgments   12

1. MIXED GENERATIONS
   Granddad Wouldn't Approve   13

2. MIXED BLESSING
   Do We Have Your Blessing?   21

3. MIXED EMOTIONS
   What Will People Think?   29

4. MIXED MOTIVES
   Why Are Your Children Trying to Hurt You?   43

5. MIXED SIGNALS
   Yellow Lights and Red Lights   59

6. MIXED UP
   Lock Your Doors   75

7. MIXED REVIEWS
   With(in) or Without   89

8. MIXED IDENTITY
   What About the Children?   111

9. MIXED SUPPORT
   After They Say, "I Do"   123

10. MIXED IMAGES
    Getting the Whole Picture   135

Glossary   151

Interracial Organizations   155

Selected Bibliography   163

Preface

Again and again we've been asked, "Why are you writing about interracial marriage?" We've asked ourselves the same question. Writing this book was the furthest thing from our minds nine years ago.

Since our family's exposure to interracial dating, we have become immersed in the topic. We found no books and only a few incidental articles on interracial marriage when we first faced a critical episode in our lives. This is not a book we wanted to write; it's a book we *had* to write.

We have talked, counseled, and wept with children and parents struggling with interracial dating issues. Our material comes from personal experience, research, and more than one hundred interviews with people directly or indirectly involved with the subject.

The general subject of our book is racism; the specific focus is interracial marriage. It is difficult to talk about interracial marriage without addressing racism. Whereas the number of interracial marriages is statistically minimal, the number of families who are personally involved is surprisingly large. Trends indicate that relatively few families will be able to avoid the issue of interracial and intercultural dating or marriage in the coming decade.

Our goal is not to promote interracial marriage, but we believe it is an issue that must be faced by society in general and Christians in particular. All marriages are "mixed" in one way or another, but interracial marriage remains one of the most volatile combinations.

We make no claims that our approach is the final or best word on the subject. Whereas we acknowledge our background as white Anglo-Saxon Protestants, our outlook has broadened beyond this limited perspective, and the Bible remains our ultimate source of authority. Whether you agree or disagree with our opinions, convictions, and conclusions, we pray that this book will become a catalyst for discussion.

In writing *Mixed Messages* the following groups of readers have been foremost in our minds:

1. individuals dating or considering dating someone of another race or culture
2. interracial and intercultural families who struggle with identity or cultural problems
3. parents, relatives, and friends of interracial couples
4. counselors, pastors, priests, and rabbis who advise couples who wish to intermarry
5. Christians who desire to confront the problem of racism and assist interracial and intercultural families

Because most of the material written on the subject of intermarriage deals with black-white marriages, the majority of our examples and statistics pertain to that type of relationship. For a large segment of the American population, interracial marriage remains a black-white issue. However, we have also discussed mixed marriages between couples of a variety of heritages, as well as between individuals who do not consider themselves to be part of any distinct racial group.

It is important that we say a word about the terminology used in our book. "Race" has become a blurred term in today's society. However, we have chosen to use the word *interracial* in our discussion. We do this not because we believe it to be the most accurate term but because the vast majority of people—including parents and grandparents—are tied emotionally to this word. "Interracial" relationships usually cause more tension and controversy than "intercultural" or "interethnic" relationships. "Intercultural" is a more inclusive term, which may or may not involve people of different races. It's possible to be married interracially and not interculturally and vice versa. For definitions of other terms, see the glossary.

According to Paul Spickard the issues are basically the same whether the marriage is considered interracial, intercultural, or interethnic. Although you may not agree with our choice of terms, our hope is that the discussion of interracial and intercultural marriage will not be overshadowed by arguments about specific words or definitions.

It is better to debate a question without settling it than to settle a question without debating it.
Joseph Joubert, 1754-1824

Acknowledgments

Numerous people have encouraged us to write this book, assuring us that we have been uniquely prepared to author it.

We would like to thank the many interracial couples and their parents who have shared their stories with us. Several people have read our manuscript, all of whom are writers and longtime acquaintances. We want to thank Harry Buerer, Jim Morud, Joseph Ryan, Karen Whitehill, and Ceilous and Mettie Williams for their suggestions and encouragement. Gloria Metz deserves special commendation. Her expertise in explaining the intricacies of word processing was invaluable.

Three organizations gave us the support we needed to complete this project: members of Temple Baptist Church of Portland, Oregon, provided a positive context for our family to grapple with the mixed messages of interracial marriage; Bethel Seminary granted Fred a sabbatical for research and writing; and Moody Press had the insight to publish a book on this controversial subject.

In addition, we would like to acknowledge our use of an excellent and timely resource, *Mixed Blood: Intermarriage and Ethnic Identity in Twentieth-Century America,* by Paul R. Spickard (Madison: U. of Wisconsin, 1989).

1

MIXED GENERATIONS
Granddad Wouldn't Approve

Our eyes focused on our son as he stood at attention in his Marine dress uniform on the hot, humid, June afternoon. A sense of pride welled up within us as we waited for Mark to take the hand of his beautiful bride and be united with her in marriage.

We thought back to the day we had attended Mark's graduation from boot camp. It had been one of the happiest days of our lives. Our son's wedding day should have been as great a celebration for us, but too much had happened in the intervening years. We were confused and bewildered. Life had not turned out as we had planned.

During his teens, Mark often made decisions without consulting us. He hadn't asked our advice when he purchased cars, dropped out of college, or joined the Marines. Although we were disappointed that Mark hadn't finished college, we had to admit that he and the Marines fit together like hand in glove. We shared Mark's pride whenever he received an honor or promotion. When Mark was stationed in England, we were excited for his opportunity to travel and experience new places and ideas.

Realizing that our three children would someday leave the nest permanently, we decided to celebrate Christmas together as a family in England the following year. Mark is our middle child, Debby our oldest, and Scott our youngest. We pictured ourselves in Dickens's romantic London with carolers singing under streetlights in the snow.

Since Mark seldom wrote letters, we didn't know what he did at the military base, if he'd made many friends in England, or whether he'd found a church to attend. But military friends assured us that there was nothing to be alarmed about and that Mark was probably doing fine. Still, we longed to spend time with him and find out how he was adjusting to military life in England.

Finally the day arrived, but our long-awaited reunion was not quite what we had expected. Mark was even more reserved as a military man, and he was no longer our "little boy." Our son was all grown up; he was a Marine. And parents' intuition quickly told us that something was bothering him. Instead of prying, however, we waited for him to get it off his chest when he was ready.

Mark dropped his bombshell after we'd been together only a few days. "I'm dating a girl over here," he told each family member separately. "Let's just say that Granddad wouldn't approve." None of us needed any further explanation. Mark was dating a black woman! Not sure what our verbal responses would convey, we each remained silent.

What do you say when traditions begin to crumble? Mark had explained his relationship matter-of-factly. "It's only a temporary thing," he told us. "When I come back to the United States in March, I'll be reassigned to a different base. It'll all be over by then."

It wasn't until Mark returned to his base the next day that the four of us discovered we'd each been told about his girlfriend the same way—"Granddad wouldn't approve." Perhaps it had been easier for Mark to tell us separately than as a group, thus avoiding a four-against-one situation.

It was hard for us to believe that Mark would consider dating someone of another race. Like his granddad, Mark's attitude toward people of other races had always been one of superiority and hostility. Since he admired his granddad's philosophy, we were baffled and totally unprepared by this sudden change of heart.

Children do not always (or even usually) select partners according to their parents' wishes. Although we knew that all three of our children would have to make their own marital decisions, we secretly hoped that they would marry "well"—perhaps choosing doctors, lawyers, professors, or even pastors.

Many fine Christian young people attended our home church at that time. If our children couldn't find Mr.—or Miss—Right there, we hoped and prayed that they would meet that special person at a youth rally, church camp, or Christian college. Unfortunately, prior to Mark's bombshell we had never discussed the search for a marriage partner with our children, other than to stress the importance of choosing a Christian. Suddenly we wished we had been more specific. We realized that interacting with children about choosing a lifetime partner is both a privilege and a responsibility.

We had teased our children about individuals in the church whom we thought would make good partners. Our youngsters once got together to decide whom each should marry. Since our church was composed of many interrelated families, they reasoned that if the three of them married into enough families, "the church could never vote to get rid of Dad as its pastor." Of course, none of these choices ever materialized.

As far as we can remember, we never discussed the subject of interracial marriage with our children. It was a nonissue. We assumed that they would eventually marry individuals of their own race. Fred's mother had often commented that "birds of a feather flock together." It was understood that casual friendships with people who were different were fine, but dating friendships and intimate relationships should be with "our kind of people."

Our children's paternal grandparents never talked about people of other races. In contrast, Anita's parents (especially her father, better known as "Granddad") were quite outspoken on the subject. Granddad had nothing good to say about people who were unlike him. Both sets of grandparents were prejudiced; the only difference was that Fred's parents avoided talking about their judgments, whereas Anita's discussed them freely and with strong conviction.

We didn't talk about the possibility that Mark would marry the woman he had told us about. We returned to the United States thinking that time and distance were on our side. Soon Mark would be reassigned to the United States, and our anguish would end.

During the next few months we heard little from Mark. Since he made no further mention of his girlfriend, we assumed that his infatuation was over. We didn't mention anything to our friends or extended family about the situation.

About 5:30 A.M. one Sunday in 1982, the telephone awakened us. It was Mark calling from England (he never seemed to realize what time it was in Oregon when he called). After exchanging greetings, Mark said, "I called to let you know I'm getting married. Do I have your blessing? We're getting married in June. Can you come to the wedding in Louisiana?" Another bombshell had caught us off guard.

The next few months dragged by. We avoided talking about the subject even to each other, hoping the wedding would be delayed until we could at least meet our future daughter-in-law. After many sleepless nights, the wedding date finally drew near, and our anxiety level became almost unbearable.

Completely unprepared for what lay ahead, we flew to New Orleans with Debby and Scott, and Mark's friend Dick rode five thousand miles on his motorcycle to support Mark in his decision. The five of us were the only "white folk" in attendance besides the groom.

Tension filled the New Orleans hotel room where we stayed the night before the wedding. We had yet to meet Mark's fiancée, Martha, or any of her family. About 9:30 that evening as we were getting ready for bed a knock came at our door. There stood Mark, Martha, and Martha's mother. During the uncomfortable hours that followed, we sought to accomplish a task that ordinarily takes place over a period of months or even years—getting acquainted.

The next day we traveled to the rural community where the wedding would take place. As directions to the wedding site were unclear, we stopped at a little country grocery store to ask if anyone knew where Martha's parents lived. One of the black customers said, "Let me show you. It's easier than trying to explain." We followed her outside, and she pointed down the road. "Drive down that way till you cross the bridge; then turn right at the white lady's house." We wondered if the "white lady" would be standing in her front yard so that we could recognize her. We began to understand that not everyone views the world from our perspective.

June 19, 1982, was one of the longest days of our lives. The outdoor wedding was scheduled to take place at 5:00 P.M. We arrived at Martha's home, the site of the wedding, shortly after noon. Everyone was busily making last-minute preparations. Pastel gowns were being hemmed, food prepared, and the yard decorated.

With the temperature and humidity both in the nineties, no one seemed anxious to get dressed in his or her wedding finery. Fred's anxiety increased another notch when he realized that there would be no rehearsal for the wedding at which he was to officiate. That wouldn't have been a problem with a simple ceremony, but this was no ordinary backyard wedding. Forty-two people made up the wedding party!

The announced time for the wedding came and went. The ceremony scheduled for 5:00 began at 6:45. (In Oregon some guests would have left had the service been more than fifteen minutes late.) An instrumental group played while people filtered in from every direction. This backyard extravaganza was to be the social event of the year for the community.

At last everything was ready. Bridesmaids and groomsmen took their places. Little girls in a rainbow of pretty dresses dropped flower petals along the path. Martha smoothed her gown and readied herself to walk down the long red carpet laid over the ground. We glanced toward Mark. He stood at attention, waiting to receive his bride. Although we were happy for Mark, we were also overwhelmed by everything that had transpired during the previous six months. We barely held back our tears.

The wedding hostess announced each attendant and family member by name over a loudspeaker as he or she entered. Both mothers were elegantly gowned, and the fathers wore tuxedos, Fred dressed in brown and Bishop Ousley, Martha's father, in white. When the band played the processional, the hostess excitedly requested, "Everybody please stand!"

We began to rise, but Martha's mother reached over and firmly admonished us. "Stay seated. You don't stand. You're not everybody; you're somebody!" We looked at each other and smiled. That important distinction helped us sort out our responses to our son's marriage, and it would help us deal with what was yet to come.

We arrived at our motel later that evening, wet with perspiration. Had we lost a son or gained a daughter-in-law? Our acquaintance with Martha spanned two short days. Would we ever get to know that shy, frightened girl? Not only were our races different, but so were our cultures. Her black, Southern, rural, Pentecostal family painted a striking contrast to our white, Northern, urban, Baptist family.

It was no longer a question of whether or not Mark and Martha *should* get married. They *were* married. Nothing would change that fact. We could either accept their marriage or allow it to cause us anguish.

After a brief honeymoon, the newlyweds flew to Portland for a second reception in our home. Sunday morning Mark and Martha were introduced to the congregation of Temple Baptist Church, where Fred was senior pastor. Relatively few of the five hundred people in attendance were aware that Mark had married a black woman, and the silence was overwhelming. We wondered what each person thought at that moment, although it was probably best that we couldn't read their minds.

Why did we have such a problem with our son's interracial marriage? Was the problem Mark's and Martha's, or was it ours? Was it a societal dilemma or an individual one? Should we be pleased or apologetic? Did we feel joy or grief?

It would be wonderful to say that our struggles ended after the wedding recessional, but we faced the issue again a few months later. But that's getting ahead of our story.

2

MIXED BLESSING
Do We Have Your Blessing?

What does it mean to have someone's blessing? It basically means receiving permission, approval, acceptance, or endorsement for a decision.

Since Fred had not asked his parents or Anita's parents for permission to marry Anita, Mark's question, "Do I have your blessing?" came as a complete surprise to us. That early Sunday morning request was an unavoidable question that demanded an answer. Although still half-asleep, Fred responded immediately. "How can I bless your marriage to a girl I've never met? I don't even know her name!"

"It's Martha. She's the girl I told you I was dating when you were here at Christmas."

"Is she a Christian, Mark?"

"Yes, she's a Christian. What's the problem?"

"Let's talk more about this when you come home next month," Anita suggested, hoping to prolong a final decision.

"You don't understand, Mom. There's nothing to talk about."

Granted, we hadn't asked for our parents' approval when we decided to get married, but we wanted to approve of our own children's marital partners. We hesitated, not only because Mark wanted to marry a woman of a different race and culture but because she was a complete stranger to us. Even though we felt helpless and frustrated, we appreciated the importance Mark placed upon our blessing.

We did not consider it theoretically or theologically wrong for our children to marry individuals of another race, but it was unthinkable that they would even consider doing so. It was very difficult for us to accept Mark's decision.

Since we had no way to call Mark in England and would not see him until shortly before the wedding, we decided to write to him regarding our misgivings. It seemed the right thing to do at the time, but in retrospect our letter probably added injury to an already fragile situation. Not only did Mark read our letter, but Martha read it as well. Our relationship with our future daughter-in-law became strained before we even met her.

We've often wondered how we could have prepared ourselves better for this traumatic turn of events. When we discussed marriage with our children, we had focused on the importance of marrying a Christian. So Mark's response to our concerns was understandable. "What's the problem? She's a Christian."

Now we wish that we had taken more time to discuss both dating relationships and marriage partnerships with our children. Before children begin dating, parents should discuss basic rules and guidelines, aside from ethnic, cultural, or racial issues.

Most parents want their children to accept people of diverse backgrounds. When friendships consistently include people who are different, it's inevitable that some of them will develop into romantic relationships. If social contact leads to a more serious relationship, how should parents respond? The way parents choose to react will affect immediate as well as long-range relationships. It is better, however, if parents consider their options before they face an actual situation. The following are some common responses.

MAKE THE CHILD FEEL GUILTY

A common response for parents is to shame a child for even considering interracial dating. The opposition may first take the form of humorous or negative remarks. If that does not persuade a child to cease dating, pressure is increased by questions intended to cause guilt. Emotional pressure can be applied by asking the following questions:

1. Don't you have any pride in your own culture or heritage?
2. How could you think so little of yourself? You can do so much better than that.
3. You know how we feel; how could you do this to us?
4. Don't you realize that if your grandmother ever finds out what you've done, it will kill her?[1]

Those escalating questions are designed to create enough guilt in the child for him or her to discontinue intercultural dating. If mental and emotional coercion don't cause the child to break off the relationship, the next possible course of action may be more drastic.

FORBID THE CHILD TO DATE INTERRACIALLY

Some parents think the best way to deal with a potential problem is to act quickly and decisively without discussing the subject. "We don't ever want you to see him again. We don't want to discuss it. This is not a suggestion. It's the law!"

Sometimes parents are justified in forbidding a child to date a certain person. Legitimate grounds for such a decision may be moral, legal, religious, and so on. (Further discussion of these criteria may be found in chapter 5.)

When the grounds are not explained or biblically based, however, a child's response may be just the opposite to what the parents desire. In fact, the more adamantly parents forbid a relationship, the stronger it may become, to the point where the couple takes it underground. When young people are forced to choose between obeying parents and continuing a romantic relationship, they often make poor choices.

Anita recently talked to a woman who had served with her husband as a missionary in Africa. They and their children had learned to know and love many black people while living there. Soon after the missionary family moved back to the United States, their nineteen-year-old daughter began to date an African-American in his early thirties.

Her parents strenuously objected to the relationship, not only because the man was black but because of the differences in their ages. However, the daughter said that she related to her black friend more easily than she did to white men. When her parents refused to meet her friend, the tensions escalated. Before long, communication was no longer possible, and the girl moved out of her home.

OSTRACIZE THE CHILD FROM THE PARENTS' CIRCLE OF FRIENDS

A woman from the East Coast telephoned Fred in desperation. "I need your help!" she pleaded. "Ten years ago I married a black man. My father, who is a Protestant minister in another state, visits us and enjoys playing with his grandchildren, but he doesn't want any of his friends or church members to know of my marriage." The woman continued to explain her predicament, saying that the parishioners didn't even know she or her family existed. "He has forbidden us to come to the town where he serves as pastor. I have accepted this arrangement all these years, but I can't live with these conditions any longer. When my grandmother died, I was not even allowed to attend her funeral."

That woman had been relegated to the position of social outcast for ten years and could no longer continue as a nonentity. While her pastor-father preached acceptance and brotherly love from the pulpit, he denied both to his own family.

Another interracially married woman, who lives in Chicago, also lamented that she had conformed to her parents' desire that she keep her marriage a secret. In an article in the *Chicago Tribune* she described her clandestine marriage. "Except for my parents and brothers and sisters, no one in my family, including my grandmother, knows that I'm even married. That's how my parents want it," she said. "Whenever we visit home, my parents meet us in a restaurant. I know they love the kids and they try to make it up materially, but they don't want us to come over. They don't want the neighbors to see us." When asked if she would have handled things differently, she said, "I'd never agree to keep quiet about my marriage. But it's too late now."[2]

SEND THE CHILD AWAY

When a child persists in dating someone of another race or culture, some parents think the only solution is a geographic one. This may be achieved in a number of ways. Perhaps the least drastic is to change churches or schools. However, with the ease of transportation and communication in modern America, that may no longer be a deterrent to most teenagers.

To send the child away to another city, state, or country is a more radical step. Parents often feel that time and distance will cool a relationship. The old adage "Absence makes the heart grow fonder" can work two ways. Time and distance will either solidify the relationship or provide a context for new relationships. (Absence can make the heart grow fonder for someone else!) If a couple is genuinely in love, being separated will not terminate the relationship or change their feelings.

COMMUNICATE, SHOW CONCERN, AND COUNSEL

Rather than acting in a harsh or precipitous manner, parents can work hard to keep the lines of communication open with their children. A cessation in communication usually results in burned bridges. However, if communication is not natural and healthy prior to a crisis, it is unlikely to develop in a wholesome manner under pressure. Children and parents need to discuss their views on marriage together, as well as with others.

According to a recent poll in *U.S.A. Today,* 86 percent of white Americans say they wouldn't mind if a black family moved next door, and 88 percent of whites wouldn't mind if their six-year-old child brought home a black playmate. However, 60 percent would disapprove if their sister started to date a black man.[3] The percentage would almost certainly be greater if white parents were asked, "Would you want your daughter to marry a black man?"

In an article written almost thirty years ago titled "My Negro Problem and Ours," Norman Podhoretz points to the challenge many parents still face when asked to give their blessing to a child who wants to marry interracially. "If I were asked today whether I would like a daughter of mine to marry [interracially] I would have to answer, 'No, I wouldn't like it at all.' I would rail and rave and tear my hair. And then I would have the courage to curse myself for raving and ranting, and then give her my blessing."[4]

Because parents don't know when their children or grandchildren might begin to date interracially or interculturally, they should prepare for that eventuality. Parents should not flippantly give or withhold their blessing, and children should regard the blessing equally seriously.

Hopefully, your answer to the question, "Do I have your blessing?" will be based on conviction, courage, honesty, and love. Some parents will "rant and rave and tear their hair"; others will curse God, themselves, their children, or all three. Thanks be to God that those are not the only options.

We learned that we had given mixed messages to our children. Because we had been silent on some issues of dating and marriage, our children had assumed that we believed that the color of one's skin or the origin of one's family didn't matter to us. What we believe theologically and theoretically was tested experientially.

NOTES

1. Janet Bode, *Different Worlds: Interracial and Cross-Cultural Dating* (New York: Franklin Watts, 1989), p. 55.
2. Lynn Emmerman, "Mixed Blessings," *Chicago Tribune*, Sunday, September 9, 1990, sec. 15.
3. Tom Squitieri, "Affirmative Action Still Divides Races," *U.S.A. Today* (September 22, 1989): 1-2.
4. In Paul R. Spickard, *Mixed Blood: Intermarriage and Ethnic Identity in Twentieth-Century America* (Madison: U. of Wisconsin, 1989), p. 294.

3

MIXED EMOTIONS
What Will People Think?

With which animal do you identify and why?" a seminar leader asked us. Although the question seemed silly at first, it proved to be an icebreaker and helped us learn more about each other.

Fred identified with the eagle because of its ability to soar high above everyone else. He desires to be able to see other people's problems without their seeing his. Anita, on the other hand, identified with a mother bear. Although she appears soft and warm on the outside, should someone threaten her children, she is ready to attack.

As we both have outgoing personalities and have a healthy degree of self-confidence, it is easy for us to relate to a variety of people. Our first twenty-five years of marriage passed with few problems or major incidents. However, that telephone call from our son in England disrupted our peaceful existence.

In fact, even our identities changed significantly in an unconscious transformation. We both climbed into our private shells. No longer were we an eagle and mother bear; now we were a pair of turtles.

The news of Mark's upcoming wedding should have brought us much joy and a desire to tell everyone we knew. Instead we grew silent and confused. Whom should we tell? How should we break the news? What reactions might we expect?

We didn't question our son's love for a woman of another race; however, *acceptance* on our part was certainly not immediate. We went about our daily responsibilities pretending all was well, only to return at the end of the day to face our anguish and confusion. Home was the only place where we felt completely free to talk about our anger and pain. Anita remembers emotions fluctuating from disappointment, to embarrassment, to anger with God.

"I wouldn't have bothered to pray if I'd have known this is how He'd answer," she cried. "How can God allow this to happen to me?" Feeling sorry for herself and agonizing over Mark's engagement, Anita lashed out at Debby and Scott one day. "Now I suppose one of you will marry a Hare Krishna, and the other will turn gay," she exclaimed. "Then I might as well jump off a bridge!"

We went through various stages of willingness to face the crisis. First we considered it a bad joke. Next we denied it, treating the situation as a temporary problem. Soon it threatened to become a permanent nightmare. Speculation shifted from the possibility of marriage, to the probability of marriage, to the inevitability of marriage. Although Debby and Scott empathized with us as we struggled, they saw no problem with interracial marriage.

For several weeks we continued to live within our protective shells, moving slowly and cautiously. Turtles tend to function in isolation rather than in colonies or flocks. They creep silently across pavement and logs, often unnoticed.

Our initial problem was one of pride. A question lurked in the back of our minds, although we never discussed it openly. "What will our family and friends think?" Parents are no different from their teenage children in their desire for approval from their friends. One father whose son was dating a girl of another race expressed his struggle this way: "Prejudice . . . comes, I believe, from parents being worried about the image that's presented to their friends. Parents . . . just like kids, want peer approval. They feel pressure to have their kids live right, go to the right schools, date right, and eventually marry right."[1]

Fred's acceptance, although not immediate, came about gradually as he studied the Scriptures and talked with Anita. Careful examination of our attitudes and emotions eventually brought us both to the realization that God had work to do in our lives. It was while reading Colossians 3:10-11 that Anita finally found peace.

> You are living a brand new kind of life that is continually learning more and more of what is right, and trying constantly to be more and more like Christ who created this new life within you. In this new life one's nationality or race or education or social position is unimportant; such things mean nothing. Whether a person has Christ is what matters, and he is equally available to all. (TLB*)

After Mark's engagement was announced, we were besieged with questions from friends and church members about the ceremony and our future daughter-in-law. "Do you have any pictures?" "How did they meet?" "Is she from England?" "Will it be a church wedding?"

We wondered how we should tell our friends that Mark's fiancée was black. Would people understand? Since our own thinking was still unclear, we doubted that others would be able to comprehend either. Did we need the support of family and friends, or did we want

The Living Bible.

their pity and comfort? Did we want to discuss the subject of interracial marriage, or did we hope it would just go away? Until we had sorted through our feelings and prejudices, we were not ready to deal with other people's reactions and opinions.

In the previous chapter we dealt with the subject of parental approval. This chapter discusses the need that parents have for peer approval. But where do they go to find it?

As turtles, we became cautious about sticking out our necks. We each decided to share our secret in a different way. If responses were favorable, we'd risk sticking out our necks a bit farther and more often. Should responses be negative, we'd retreat into our shells and wait until it seemed safe again.

At the time, neither of us was well acquainted with couples whose children had married African-Americans. Anita decided to share her secret with a friend who knew nothing about the girl Mark planned to marry. Her friend's son had married a woman of another racial background, so Anita asked, "How are you handling your son's marriage?"

"Oh, we like her all right," the woman replied. "At least she's not black!" Back into its shell popped Anita's head.

But she eventually decided to try sharing her predicament again. Fortunately, this time her audience listened attentively and gave Anita the courage and confidence to tell others. When Anita confided in a friend of Chinese descent, it did not occur to her until afterward that the woman herself was intermarried. Yet, her friend listened patiently and told Anita about painful reactions she'd encountered to her own marriage.

The first person Fred told was a black pastor friend. "I need to talk to you about something that has happened in our family," Fred said. "Our son recently informed us that he's getting married to a black woman."

"Well," his friend answered, "our daughter recently told us that she is pregnant and wants to marry her white boyfriend. My response was one of anger," he continued. "When I found this young man, I told him, 'If it wasn't for the fact that I am a Christian, I would probably kill you!'" Although his friend's response shocked Fred, it was good to know that we weren't the only parents who had trouble dealing with the possibility of intermarriage.

No one on either side of our family, as far as we knew, had ever married interracially. Although our nearest relatives lived more than one thousand miles away, we knew they'd have to be told sooner or later. Anita decided not to tell her aging, invalid parents about Mark's marriage. She thought the shock would have been too much for them to handle. Both of her parents died within months of the wedding, never having seen a picture of their grandson's bride.

Fred's relatives found out about Mark's marriage quite unexpectedly. After attending his brother's funeral service, Fred sat in a living room with about twenty-five other guests. A relative from the South had learned of the approaching wedding but had no idea who Mark was going to marry. "Tell Mark I'm glad he's marrying a white woman!" he called across the room in a loud voice. Fred groped for words. After a brief pause, he responded, "I could tell Mark that, but she's black." Instantly, conversation ceased. At first some of the relatives and guests thought Fred was joking. Others appeared confused. A few were outright shocked. One thing was certain—the man who used that expression will never use it again!

Do you volunteer information about your children if they are dating or have married someone of another race or culture? Do you mention race or culture as you mention other characteristics, such as age, occupation, education, religious affiliation, background, and so on? Or do you avoid the subject completely unless someone asks you a specific question? There is no universally correct way or proper time to share this information.

Determine beforehand what your attitude will be, regardless of how others respond. The insight of a friend was extremely helpful to us: "Your friends will understand; your enemies don't matter." We found that to be true. The more we shared our secret, the better we felt and the more support we received.

Early in our pilgrimage we decided to share our story with others who also were wrestling with the question of interracial relationships. People encouraged us to write about our experiences, especially because there seemed to be little written on the subject from a Christian perspective. An article published in 1987 in *The Standard,* a denominational magazine, received an overwhelmingly positive response. Someone wisely cautioned us, however, to wait a few years before attempting to write a book on the subject, to give the wounds and bruises an opportunity to heal.

Over the past nine years we have learned that as parents of white children we have only one perspective. There are many roles in this real-life drama to be explored and understood. In talking to other parents whose children are in interracial relationships, we have discovered four basic reactions among parents.

REACTIONS

DENIAL

Many families treat the subject of interracial marriage as they treated divorce a generation ago. Fred's family never discussed the fact that several of his relatives had been divorced. Only years later did he find out that these family members had committed the "unmentionable and unpardonable sin." Anita was twelve years old before she learned that her father had been married previously and that she had a half-brother eight years older than she. Divorce was simply not discussed in nice circles.

Some parents also deny the existence of an interracial marriage. No pictures of the couple appear around the house or in the purse or wallet. They remain out of sight, hidden in a piano bench or a dresser drawer.

Even after the couple has married, parents refuse to accept or even discuss the marriage. When Anita inquired of a friend how things had gone at her daughter's recent interracial wedding, the woman pulled her aside and quietly told her, "I don't want to talk about it here. No one other than you folks knows about the wedding."

APOLOGETIC

"You'll never believe what happened to us this week. Our daughter informed us that she is getting married to a Native American." Parents who share information in this manner are often looking for sympathy. Interracial marriage and dating is one of the few remaining taboos in our society. To some people it is scandalous and belongs in the same category as daughters who bear children out of wedlock or children who choose a gay lifestyle.

These parents react to the possibility of an interracial in-law and biracial grandchildren with grief. It becomes an all-consuming issue in their thoughts and conversation.

ACCEPTANCE

"Our son is dating a Puerto Rican girl. We don't like the idea, but it's his life and his decision. We don't approve of the relationship, but we might as well accept it." Parents taking this approach want people to know that their son or daughter has done something they don't approve of, even though they give verbal assent. Their nonverbal signals and tone of voice indicate disapproval. These parents don't want to be considered old-fashioned, bigoted, or racist, so their neutral comments cover up their emotional responses to their child's decision.

SUPPORTIVE

"All parents, motivated by love, concern and a deep desire to protect [their children] push for a course of action that they believe will lead to the fewest complications," said New York City therapist Ronny Diamond.[2]

Our lives became increasingly complicated when we tried to include our daughter-in-law and her relatives in our family circle. We had to decide how we'd fit our expanded family into our existing circle of friends. Would our new family structure increase or decrease the quantity and quality of our other relationships?

Although the number of interracial and intercultural marriages will certainly grow in coming years, society will not automatically approve of these unions. Individual approval depends on personal contact with people who are intermarried. A person's position will be supported (or undermined) by examples of people who are interracially married. For instance, if an individual knows of several mixed marriages that have failed or mixed families where children suffer from a lack of identity, his or her attitude will probably be negative.

On the other hand, if he is aware of successful interracial marriages with well-adjusted biracial children, he will probably be supportive.

In spite of the tendency people have to predict the success or failure of an interracial marriage, there is no way to determine how healthy that marriage would be if the same two individuals were of identical races and cultures. Whenever one travels down a seldom-used path, or decides to carve out a new one, the risks increase. Most interracial families who support and love one another believe adversity has made them stronger.

As we shared our secret with friends and family we discovered a variety of viewpoints regarding the advisability of mixed marriages. More and more people are being forced to deal with this subject on a personal level. Each viewpoint is affected by many factors: personal experience, peer approval, perception of other racial groups, exposure to mixed families, and so on.

VIEWPOINTS

We should be willing to change our attitudes, based on education and exposure. Discussion should transcend the academic and ethereal and move to theological and ethical considerations. Whereas there are many opinions on interracial marriages, we think there are four basic viewpoints. Two are favorable and two are unfavorable.

APPROVAL AS NORMAL AND HEALTHY

Even though few individuals or groups regard intermarriage as a social goal, several groups promote it as a step toward the unity of the human race.

On a purely biological basis, some believe that all living organisms—plants, animals, and humans—are strengthened by mixing different strains within the species. Those who hold this view believe cross-racial or cross-cultural marriages produce "stronger" offspring.

Others who approve of intermarriage as normal and healthy view mixing as the only way to achieve equality. "The call to marriage in black and white is essential because it is the only way in which blacks can be fully and unreservedly accepted by whites and the only way in which whites can be fully accepted by blacks," states Joseph Washington, the author of *Marriage in Black and White.*[3]

To our knowledge, no religious group promotes intermarriage as a basic tenet. However, the Baha'i religion comes close to espousing this view, teaching that interracial marriage is a service to humankind. Because Baha'i emphasizes unity within the human race, adherents believe intermarriage helps relieve racial tension and therefore is a step toward achieving oneness.

ACCEPTANCE AS SPECIAL AND UNIQUE

Some people maintain that marriage should be only between those who are similar because marriage itself is subject to many obstacles. This philosophy could be summed up, "The fewer the impediments, the better." These people say a marriage has a better chance of success when the partners have as many characteristics in common as possible. Similar ethnic backgrounds, educations, social standings, religious beliefs, racial identities, and values lessen the tensions in the relationship.

Those who espouse this view hold to the equality of all people as well as individual freedom to choose a marriage partner; nonetheless, they claim the best marital union is one between similar people. Interracial couples take a special, unique path when they go against the norms of society. When they make such a choice, they should be accepted, respected, and admired for their willingness to live with the consequences of "bucking the system."

The Reverend C. Eugene Askew supports this opinion in an article titled "Should My Daughter Marry a Negro?":

> I hope [my children] will seek suitable dates and/or marriage partners among young people most like themselves religiously, culturally, economically and racially. But if our children and circumstance decide otherwise, my wife and I hereby pledge love and understanding to them, their mates, their in-laws, their friends, and grandchildren.[4]

The problems and pressures of society continue to be strong hindrances to those who seek to travel this isolated and "dangerous" path. Mixed couples may acknowledge that the obstacles exist, but they don't see them as permanent or insurmountable barriers. Once they make a choice to take the risk, those who hold to the "unique relationship" viewpoint willingly accept and support that decision.

OPPOSED AS QUESTIONABLE AND PROBLEMATIC

Some people say interracial marriages cause too many problems and raise too many questions. They base this reasoning on sociological or cultural dynamics, not the superiority of a specific race or ethnic group.

Many forces may prevent or destroy a mixed marriage. Among the most powerful are economic and relational. The people most able to offer interracial couples support—parents, family, and friends—may have strong reservations about intermarriage. They may think that although the couple seems to be compatible and is willing to face the opposition, the children they bear will have no choice. Mixed children supposedly suffer from lack of identity, racial slurs, and stereotypes. In addition, interracial families are often discriminated against in employment and housing, even though such practices are illegal.

Those in the "too questionable" camp claim that society still doubts the motives of interracial couples and that too many people will be negatively affected by their decision to marry. No matter how sincere the couple may be, many claim it is not worth the cost.

REJECTED AS NEUROTIC AND DESTRUCTIVE

This view is held by a blend of people with differing philosophies; however, all agree on one thing—that interracial and intercultural marriage is wrong. Some hold that any mixing of the races, especially through marriage, weakens the races. Races (especially the white race) need to remain separate to protect the purity of the blood. Groups such as white supremacists, the Ku Klux Klan, and skinheads reject interracial marriage on this basis.

Other groups, including minorities, maintain that interracial and intercultural marriage will eventually mean the loss of identity, or cultural suicide. In the 1960s, black militants began to stress the need for separation of the races and cultures to prevent assimilation into a dominant society. Not only African-Americans but also members of other races, especially recent immigrants, believe it is essential to maintain cultural ties with their place of origin. They claim intermarriage weakens or destroys identity.

Even the best opinions are tested when the decision becomes a personal one. No one can escape the question that defies reason or logic: "Would you want your daughter to marry one?" Most people answer that question with a simple yes or no. However, it can also be answered with another question: "Which one did you have in mind?"

Marriage is an institution ordained by God. He provided for men and women to come together to enjoy life and to bring children into the world. As each person considers whether to marry and whom to marry, God's blessing and guidance becomes clear. Because of the significance of the marital choice, the couple should have their families' and society's blessing.

Our prayer for all couples is that they choose God's best, regardless of racial or cultural barriers. May our message be clear on this subject.

As we attempted to sort through the implications of our son's marriage, we decided to watch a rerun of a film on television that dealt with our dilemma. We viewed "Guess Who's Coming to Dinner?" from a totally different perspective than we ever had before. The film, produced in the late 1960s, stars Katharine Hepburn and Sidney Poitier and centers on the courtship of an interracial couple and the effect of that relationship on their families. Although many complications in the couple's relationship were meant to be entertaining, we no longer perceived them as funny. What was once a humorous incident for a fictitious family had ceased to be a joke.

Who will come to dinner at our house? we wondered. Now that a new member from another race and culture had joined our family, would previous relationships be affected?

Dinner and other social events might still have their humorous moments, but we no longer were dealing with comedy; it was reality. To our surprise, our friendships gained strength once we decided to be positive and supportive of our new daughter-in-law.

NOTES

1. Janet Bode, *Different Worlds: Interracial and Cross-Cultural Dating* (New York: Franklin Watts, 1989), p. 49.
2. Ibid., p. 54.
3. Joseph R. Washington, Jr., *Marriage in Black and White* (Boston: Beacon, 1971), pp. 326-27.
4. C. Eugene Askew, "Should My Daughter Marry a Negro?" in *Marrying Across the Color Line,* ed. Cloyte M. Larsson (Chicago: Johnson, 1965), p. 33.

4

MIXED MOTIVES

Why Are Your Children
Trying to Hurt You?

It had been a long, hot summer. Mark's marriage had stretched us emotionally and spiritually. While still somewhat overwhelmed by our son's marriage, we were forced to face another trauma.

Our daughter, Debby, spent her last year of college in New York City at the tender age of twenty-two. Working in the publishing and fashion world, Debby met people from many levels of society. Whereas her parents' growing up years had been sheltered and their relationships with different people minimal, Debby enjoyed exposure to much diversity. She had already lived in ten houses and seven different states, from New England to the Pacific Northwest, in contrast to her parents, who had lived in the same hometown for twenty years. Although we didn't realize all the pressures Debby faced, we were confident she could handle herself. We trusted her and the decisions she made.

Although separated by the width of a continent, Debby remained a source of encouragement to us with her frequent letters and telephone calls. We always looked forward to the times when she could fly to Portland to visit. Both Debby and her brother Scott helped us to see that we needed to do everything possible to support Mark in his marriage decision.

That August, two months after Mark and Martha's wedding, Debby returned to the Pacific Northwest to be a bridesmaid in the wedding of a college classmate. Afterward, she came home to spend a few days with us. Flowers awaited her arrival. Debby beamed with excitement as she opened the slender white box and admired the long-stemmed roses inside.

"They're from Bruce!" she said as she read the enclosed card.

"Who is Bruce?" we asked.

"He's the guy who escorted me down the aisle at Sue and Terry's wedding. He and Terry were best friends at Harvard."

She proceeded to pull some snapshots from her purse. "Here he is," she said as she handed us a picture. "He's the one standing next to me."

We looked at each other in disbelief as Debby pointed to her escort. Bruce was black! We were too stunned to be upset. Could it be possible that our daughter had also fallen in love with someone of another race?

The year had been a traumatic one. In addition to Mark's engagement in March, followed by his June wedding, we were disappointed to learn that Scott would not be participating in the commencement ceremonies of his high school class. Throughout the summer Anita made repeated trips to the Midwest to assist her elderly parents. It was upon Anita's return from her mother's funeral that she learned about Debby's romance.

But perhaps we were getting ahead of ourselves. After all, Debby and Bruce had just met the previous weekend. We reminded ourselves that our children had had many infatuations and would probably have many more. Besides, Bruce was a law student on the East

Coast, and Debby planned to move back to Portland, so why worry? Although we didn't know how we'd handle the prospect of another interracial marriage, we knew that Debby would give us time to get acquainted with Bruce before she made a major decision.

Debby was still "Daddy's little girl." No boy she had ever dated had been quite good enough. In fact, to her father, they all seemed like "jerks." But Bruce was special. Over the next two years we spent holidays and vacation time together with the two of them and gradually grew to know and appreciate Bruce as a person.

"When I listed all the qualities I wanted in a husband, I never thought to write down *white*," Debby told us as we discussed the romance, which was taking a serious turn. "Bruce meets all the qualities I'm looking for in a husband."

We had to admit that Bruce was a fine young man. He was a Christian and had a good education and a promising career as a lawyer. His value system, interests, and goals seemed similar to Debby's. Once again, our major concern was his race. Theologically and theoretically, we couldn't see why we shouldn't approve of a wedding. But emotionally and spiritually, we still had to deal with our prejudices and stereotypes.

Parents of minority children also struggle with accepting their children's choices of white partners. When our daughter became engaged to an African-American, her fiancé's mother could not understand why her son couldn't find a black woman to marry.

Why was this such a struggle for us again? Mark and Debby seemed very happy. Martha and Bruce were both Christians. But we continued to be troubled. Mark's question returned to us again and again, "What's the problem, Dad?"

Again we wrestled with emotions, admitting that even though we would have preferred that our children choose mates from our church, neighborhood, economic and education background, and ethnic heritage, they had the right to make their own decisions, just as we had made ours more than twenty-five years before.

Debby and Bruce planned a traditional church wedding, to be held in our home church in Oregon, where Fred was senior pastor. It was a gala affair, as Mark and Martha's wedding had been. Both weddings were unique in that they were each the first black-white wedding to be held in either place.

The church was full for the beautiful candlelight ceremony, the first interracial wedding most of the guests had ever seen. Friends showed their support for the newlyweds and offered much loving encouragement to a pastor and wife who were still working through their emotions.

Now that two of our children had married interracially, we had to deal with a nagging question: "What did we do wrong?" A pastor friend told us of a comment someone had made to him when he heard about our children's marriages. "I can understand it happening to them once, but how could it happen twice? What on earth did they do wrong?"

Should we have talked to our children and warned them about the dangers of interracial marriage? Did our silence indicate to them that it was OK with us? Our parents had never discussed the matter with us. Not only did they think it unacceptable; they believed it was wrong for races to mix. Although we had both grown up near racially mixed Chicago, we never knew anyone who was interracially married.

Fred's only exposure to an interracial relationship had come when a girl from his home church dated a black African student whom she met at a Christian college. When school authorities realized the relationship was getting serious, they gave the girl a choice. "Either you stop dating this man, or you leave school," they told her. Neither of them went back to the college, but Fred never learned whether they had married.

Even though our children went to high school with students of other racial backgrounds, they never dated outside of their own race. Was it just a coincidence that they married African-Americans? We continued to search for answers to these questions long after Debby's wedding.

"Why are your children trying to hurt you?" someone asked us once, referring to our children's interracial marriages. Her penetrating question had never entered our minds before, as we had not sensed that malice had been the motivation behind either marriage. But we did begin to wonder why *anyone* would want to marry interracially.

How rare is interracial marriage, particularly black-white marriage, in the United States? Statistics indicate that although marriages between black and white individuals are still a small percentage, the number has increased dramatically over the past three decades as reported by the U. S. Census Bureau (table 1).

Table 1   Interracial Marriages in the United States by Year

Year	Cumulative Total Marriages (round numbers)	Black/White	Percentages
1960	40,491,000	51,000	.01
1970	44,597,000	65,000	.01
1980	49,714,000	166,000	.03
1988	52,613,000	218,000	.04

According to the 1990 Statistical Abstract of the United States, the total number of interracial marriages has increased from 310,000 in 1970 to 956,000 in 1988.

Interracial and intercultural marriages continue to multiply at a rapid rate.

REASONS PEOPLE MARRY INTERRACIALLY

The question still remains, "Why do people marry interracially or cross-culturally?" The answer should be studied from *demographic, historical, social,* and *psychological* perspectives, all of which combine to create a total picture.

DEMOGRAPHIC

Demographically, our country has seen a new surge of immigrants in recent years. An article in *Time* describes the increase in the percentage of black and Latino students in the public school system of many large cities.[1] The statistics in that article are summed up in table 2.

Table 2   Black and Latino Students in Major U.S. Cities

City	Percentage of Students
Boston	63
Chicago	83
Houston	81
Los Angeles	75
Miami	75
New York	72
St. Louis	76

In addition, the Asian population has increased significantly in many of these cities and other cities on the West Coast.[2] This trend will affect every aspect of society, including politics, education, culture, and marriage.

With demographic changes come a change of color, and color plays an important role in many discussions of intermarriage. Because racial divisions based on anthropological and scientific distinctions are unclear, outward characteristics become important. When some people discuss interracial marriage, color is the primary issue. We have been asked the same question regarding our daughter- and son-in-law, as well as our grandchildren: "How dark are they?"

Whereas skin color is still a volatile issue, our country is currently going through a period that *Time* calls "the browning of America." By the middle of the twenty-first century, minority populations will outnumber whites in this country. That means that the number of non-Hispanic whites will have declined from 90 percent of the population in 1955 to less than 50 percent by 2055.[3] And within the next thirty years, the U.S. Census Bureau projects that the non-Hispanic white population will decrease to less than 70 percent.

This trend will inevitably impact the future mixing of races and ethnic groups in America. In some areas of the country, the available marriage partners within one's own group will be extremely limited. Many who would be personally opposed to interracial marriage will be forced to become more tolerant because of demographics. However, demographics alone will not answer the question, "Why would anyone want to marry into a different group?"

HISTORICAL

Several historical events have brought whites and nonwhites together. When immigration from Europe slowed during the early part of the twentieth century, black people migrated to Northern industrial cities in search of employment. World War II helped to break down segregation in the military, and soldiers of all races married European and Asian "war brides." The civil rights movement, coupled with the 1967 repeal of antimiscegenation laws, made social contact between races easier in the 1950s and 1960s.

SOCIAL

Social changes also affect decisions to intermarry. We can expect social walls to continue to crumble, just as we've seen political walls tumble in recent years. With more freedom to move within and between countries, it will become easier for different people groups to be exposed to others. Changes in social structure continue to influence the frequency and future of intermarriage significantly.

Several theories about social structure help explain intermarriage. In *Mixed Blood*, Paul Spickard summarizes theories that seek to explain social and economic factors that encourage intermarriage.[4]

1. *An unbalanced ratio of sexes leads to out-marriage.* Due to immigration patterns, war, slavery, and so on, there have been many cases throughout history where members of a minority group could not find partners from their own people. Even today this theory may account for a surprising new trend in the United States. In 1980, forty-five thousand black females married white males. In 1988, the number increased to sixty-nine thousand. During those eight years, white male/black female marriages increased at a faster rate than black male/ white female unions. There are fewer black males than black females in this country, particularly in professional occupations. According to the 1980 Census Bureau, 66 percent of employed black professionals were women. (In any given section of the United States this pattern may be altered, depending on the size of the minority community.)

2. *American society has become more open to racial and cultural heterogeneity.* Social change in the first half

of the twentieth century occurred slowly. In the past two decades, however, the pace has accelerated. In a Gallup poll of the general population, 4 percent approved of white/nonwhite marriage in 1958, 20 percent approved in 1968, 36 percent in 1978, and 43 percent in 1983. The black population showed an even higher degree of approval: 58 percent approved in 1972, 66 percent in 1978, and 71 percent in 1983.

The respondent's age may determine the level of his or her acceptance. In 1983 only 18 percent who were over 65 approved of black/white marriage; 32 percent of those between 50 and 64 approved; 45 percent of those between 30 and 49 approved; and 63 percent under 30 approved.[5]

No doubt the approval rate is even greater today if that trend has continued. As the older generation dies and the average level of education increases, acceptance will accelerate at an even faster rate.

As the prevalence of interracial couples increases, people will become accustomed to seeing diverse marital combinations and cease to treat them as abnormal or unusual. That does not mean, however, that everyone will approve of interracial marriage on a personal level.

It is important to note that the statistics appear to reflect an extremely high rate of approval because there is a difference between philosophical and personal approval. In a 1975 poll, white women were asked if they would accept and approve of their daughter marrying a black man. Only 14 percent said they would both accept and approve, 32 percent said they would accept but not approve, and 44 percent said they would neither accept nor approve.[6]

As people change, they may view certain racial and ethnic groups as acceptable, but their order of preference for mates will probably remain the same. Even though the number of "acceptable" groups may increase, there will probably still be a line between those who are considered "us" and those who are classified as "them."[7]

The following list is an example of ethnic preferences that might guide a Swedish American in choosing a mate. Although the order of preference may remain the same today, the number of acceptable groups has increased:

Swede
Other Scandinavian
British or German
Other White Protestant
White Catholic: German or Irish
White Catholic: Southern or Eastern European
Jew
Asian
Native American
Hispanic
Black[8]

3. *Successive generations are more willing to consider intermarriage.* During the nineteenth and twentieth centuries, most European immigrants were oppressed and persecuted when they arrived in this country. Little bound the various groups together, even though they came here for many of the same reasons. The two main points that they agreed upon were their desire to be assimilated into the American culture and that black people were beneath them on the social ladder.

But over the years, successive generations demonstrated an increasing openness toward relationships with persons of other races. Few first-generation immigrants intermarried; more second-generation intermarried; and even more third-generation intermarried.

Table 3   Black Intermarriage Hierarchy

	Before 1865	1865–1950	After 1960
Acceptable	Same status (slave/free)	Elaborate color/ status hierarchy	American Black
	African	Same region of origin	West Indian
Conceivable but unlikely	Native American	Other Black (West Indian, African)	African White Other
Nearly inconceivable	White Other	White Native American Other	

SOURCE: Paul R. Spickard, *Mixed Blood: Intermarriage and Ethnic Identity in Twentieth-Century America* (Madison: U. of Wisconsin, 1989), p. 355. By permission of The University of Wisconsin Press.

Table 4   Japanese American Intermarriage Hierarchy

	1st generation	2d generation	3d generation
Acceptable	Same village Same prefecture Japanese	Japanese	Japanese Chinese White
Conceivable but unlikely	White Chinese Okinawan Eta	White Chinese	Filipino Black
Nearly inconceivable	Filipino Black	Filipino Black	

SOURCE: Paul R. Spickard, *Mixed Blood: Intermarriage and Ethnic Identity in Twentieth-Century America* (Madison: U. of Wisconsin, 1989), p. 354. By permission of The University of Wisconsin Press.

Table 5   Chinese American Intermarriage Hierarchy

	1st generation	2d generation
Acceptable	Same village/district	Speaker of same Chinese language
	Speaker of same dialect	Speaker of another Chinese language
	Speaker of same Chinese language	Japanese
	Same province/geog. region	
		White
Conceivable but unlikely	Speaker of another Chinese language	
	White	Korean
	Japanese	Filipino
	Korean	
		Mexican
Nearly inconceivable	Filipino	Black
	Mexican	
	Black	

SOURCE: Paul R. Spickard, *Mixed Blood: Intermarriage and Ethnic Identity in Twentieth-Century America* (Madison: U. of Wisconsin, 1989), p. 354. By permission of The University of Wisconsin Press.

Our children are examples of this pattern. They are the fourth generation of European immigrants. Mark and Debby did something that their great-grandparents would never have considered, their grandparents would have disapproved of, and their parents reluctantly consented to.

4. *Social and economic class is a factor.* Although no statistics are available to prove that certain classes of people intermarry more than others, some believe that the "college educated, intellectually and artistically inclined stratum of people . . . are likely to intermarry."[9] People who intermarry are likely to be older than those who don't and living some distance from the state of their birth. Mobility and education increase the likelihood of intermarriage.

5. *Changing family structure makes intermarriage more likely.* Nothing has had a greater influence on society than the changes that have taken place within the family. The traditional picture of a man and woman with two or more children, all of the same race and culture, has undergone radical revision. The increase in single-parent families has been tremendous. Many individuals now marry a second time. Second marriages are more likely to be interracial than are first marriages. When that happens, the children of blended families have firsthand exposure to different races and cultures.

Another marked change that already has had a significant impact on the number of interracial marriages is the increase in transracial adoptions. Most transracial adoptions involve white parents and children from Africa, Asia, and Central or South America. A large number of these children will marry partners from a different race but from the same culture. They will tend to marry people with whom they share social, economic, and educational backgrounds but who have vastly different ethnic origins.

PSYCHOLOGICAL

Psychological theories, which are usually speculative, are sometimes repeated and believed as facts. Some people view interracial marriage as a neurotic, abnormal act. Ernest Porterfield discusses six theories of black-white selection: hostility, idealism, rejection, rebellion, degradation, and sex.[10] Remember, these are negative psychological theories for intermarriage.

Hostility. An individual who desires control or revenge toward another culture may choose a spouse of a different race. The hostility may result from a personal experience or an injury committed against one's own race.

Idealism. In order to prove he or she is not bigoted, an individual may marry interracially. It may be a way to act out pity for the underdog.

Rejection. Some people do not fit into the social patterns of their own ethnic group or culture. In some ways they appear to be "social misfits." Both partners could be making statements of mutual rejection of the mores and customs of their ethnic groups.

Rebellion. The nature and intensity of parental authority sometimes becomes a strong factor behind an interracial marriage. Children who have been controlled all their lives by domineering parents use marriage as a way to fight back. If a child is of legal age, he can marry against his parents' wishes to escape their authority, which he views as oppressive.

Degradation. Individuals who have low self-esteem and have been "put down" repeatedly by members of their own race may turn to someone of another race in a search for special attention. This theory has been given to explain why white prostitutes often work for a black pimp. Therapist Ronny Diamond made this comment: "In the sixties the feeling was that it was mostly liberal, white, middle class girls going out with 'black dudes,' so to speak; blacks who were not middle class. There was a sense that those kinds of girls didn't value themselves very highly. They had poor self-esteem. It had to do with the concept of 'dating or marrying down.'"[11]

Sexual. We received a telephone call from a West Coast couple whose daughter was considering marriage to a black man. The young man appeared to be a fine prospect for marriage, except that he was black. The girl's mother accepted the relationship, but her father struggled. "I'm a truck driver," he said, "and you know what kind of talk I hear at truck stops." Some young people are drawn to the adventure and temptation of the "forbidden fruit" of another race.

All the psychological theories have a degree of credence in that some individuals do marry for one or more of the preceding reasons. However, those theories are speculative and dangerous because they can be used to stereotype interracial and intercultural marriage.

None of the theories of demographics, history, social, or psychological factors deals with a primary motivation for intermarriage—love.

"In interracial marriages, one always looks for ulterior motives," says Robert Staples, a black San Francisco psychiatrist. "It is said that people marry interracially because of rebellion against their parents, sexual curiosity and other psychological reasons. But many marriages that are homogeneous take place for the same reasons. . . . People may marry their own kind for the most weird reasons, yet those reasons do not make each marriage suspect."[12]

It is difficult to separate healthy and normal motives from neurotic and abnormal ones. A marriage may take place for wrong reasons and not only survive but even flourish. All motives—positive and negative—can be applied to in-group marriages as well. Marriages that survive the forces that seek to undermine them are built on love and commitment. Because of society's negative images and prejudices against mixed marriage, interracial couples must work hard to make their marriages succeed.

Perhaps the question, "What did they do wrong?" could be restated. A young woman recently asked Anita a different question that helped put things in better perspective: "How did you train your children to be so open and accepting of people of other races?"

NOTES

1. Ezra Brown, "Getting Tough," *Time* (February 1, 1988): 52-58.
2. Ibid.
3. William A. Henry III, "Beyond the Melting Pot," *Time* (April 9, 1990): 28-31.
4. Paul R. Spickard, *Mixed Blood: Intermarriage and Ethnic Identity in Twentieth-Century America* (Madison: U. of Wisconsin, 1989), p. 69.
5. "Do You Approve or Disapprove of Marriage Between Blacks and Whites?" Princeton, N.J.: Gallup Poll, April 29–May 2, 1983. Opinion poll.
6. Spickard, *Mixed Blood*, pp. 293-94.
7. Ibid., pp. 371-72.
8. Ibid., p. 354.
9. Ibid., p. 7.
10. Ernest Porterfield, *Black and White Mixed Marriages* (Chicago: Nelson-Hall, 1978), pp. 59-84.
11. Janet Bode, *Different Worlds: Interracial and Cross-Cultural Dating* (New York: Franklin Watts, 1989), p. 81.
12. Spickard, *Mixed Blood*, p. 313.

5

MIXED SIGNALS
Yellow Lights—Red Lights

Getting married is like crossing a busy street. If there is no signal light, you can take a chance and run across the pavement. But there's usually some type of signal or warning light at main intersections. Most people are familiar with traffic lights: yellow indicates caution; red means to stop; and green says go ahead. In a specific setting you may or may not want to obey the lights, but it is always wise to heed them before proceeding.

Many couples refuse to discuss others' objections to interracial marriage. They say they are "in love, and that is enough." In her book *A New Land to Live In*, Francislee Osseo-Asare outlines a typical response of pairs who blindly decide to proceed with interracial marriage: "I was in love and all barriers seemed unimportant compared to the immensity of joy and excitement opened by our discovery of each other. I preferred trusting in the love passage of 1 Corinthians 13 to reflecting on Jesus' words about counting the cost before building a tower or going into a battle."[1]

Every couple should be willing to discuss their differences honestly and openly. Dissimilarity is not always bad or wrong. The question is, how much difference can a marital union endure and still hope for success?

While traveling in the Middle East one day we came upon a strange sight. We were journeying by horseback through a narrow rock corridor to the ancient walled city of Petra, Jordan. The setting was about as far removed from our American culture as can be imagined. To our amazement we noticed that people were living in caves high above the canyon floor. Our attention was drawn to laundry hanging out to dry and a television antenna towering above one of the caves. When we asked our tour guide, "Who lives there?" he informed us that the dwellers were an American wife and her Arab husband. We wondered how a marriage could survive such opposite cultures and worlds. What hope did that couple have for a healthy and lasting marriage?

How different is *too* different? Intermarriage may mean interfaith, intercultural, interethnic, international, or interracial. Some marriages may include all of these differences. For optimists the light will always be green if the couple is in love. For pessimists the light is always red.

Ernest Porterfield further describes these opposing views in *Black and White Mixed Marriages*: "Intermarriages are thought to be progressive endeavors by courageous, idealistic and strong human beings. This is a view held by optimists. Such unions are unhealthy liaisons entered into by maladjusted neurotics, according to the pessimists."[2]

Our goal is to examine pertinent issues in order to give guidance to couples considering interracial or intercultural marriage. We hope that our discussion will help couples more knowledgeably face the inevitable tensions.

The remainder of this chapter has been divided into three sections: yellow lights, red lights, and green lights. Some readers will see these as guiding lights; for others they will be warning lights. We view them as caution lights. Not everyone will agree that the lights are necessary. Some will question the relevance of certain issues. Others will disagree with the color category under which we have placed a particular item. Our desire is to present several categories and let each reader determine their validity and placement in his or her own life.

YELLOW LIGHTS

Time rarely heals all differences. Prejudices, stereotypes, and ethnocentrism need to be recognized and discussed because they do not simply go away. Partners not only need to recognize differences but also to be willing to deal with them. It may be best to confront some issues as they occur while maintaining a sense of humor in regard to others. Total agreement is not always the goal. Couples should be able to disagree agreeably. When Mrs. Billy Graham was asked if she agreed with her husband on everything she replied, "No. If two people agree on everything, one of them isn't necessary."

Yellow lights may be present in relationships where backgrounds are similar, but they are intensified when they are part of a culture's group psyche. The existence of yellow lights does not mean that an interracial or intercultural marriage cannot proceed. They are simply indications that a couple should allow sufficient time and make intentional effort to resolve or accept their differences. What can be a potential obstacle may actually become a stepping-stone to a mutually enriching relationship.

ROLES

Every culture establishes roles for males and females in marriage. Although the roles are not necessarily written down, they are clearly understood. We are all products of our environment; thus our roles position us in relationships. Some cultures support egalitarian interaction; in other cultures one spouse always plays a dominant role. These roles are affected by society's dominant mores and customs, especially when one of the partners is a recent immigrant to this country. Although disagreements sometimes center on important decisions, role conflicts are more likely to surface in routine matters of daily living.

VALUES

Some cultures place prime importance on the acquisition of objects—houses, appliances, clothing, money, and so on. Other cultures believe interpersonal relationships deserve primary attention. Another group may place the highest value on an individual's relationship to his or her culture. When values become a nonnegotiable part of a person's identity rather than a preference, tension is inevitable.

TIME

Fred's father considered the clock to be his companion. Anita's father treated the clock as an intruder. Fred's family always arrived early to Sunday school. Anita's family never got to Sunday school until after it had started. Time, for Fred's family, was an absolute; for Anita's family it was merely a guideline.

Time is a cultural issue, not a racial one. In Japan, for example, people literally set their watches by the departure of trains and buses, whereas in the Philippines the buses and jeepneys leave whenever the driver is ready. People usually view time from one of two perspectives: cyclical or linear. Adherents to a cyclical view of time find that opportunity arises on a regular basis. "If it isn't seized now, there will be another chance in the future," they say. Those who view time from a linear perspective believe that if an occasion is missed or forgotten, it cannot be retrieved. The opportunity is lost forever.

FAMILY RELATIONSHIPS

Some cultures have a close-knit family system. They are closely tied not only to one another but to previous generations as well. All family members may live in the same house, and there is a clear understanding of the hierarchy of authority.

Such an arrangement presents special problems when extended families and in-laws live in the same community as the couple. Privacy may be at a premium for these couples.

The following questions are important to consider: Who makes the decisions for the family? Who is the provider? Who disciplines the children? What is the process and direction of communication?

FOOD

One woman who married interracially struggled with the daily menu. Potatoes had been served at almost every evening meal in her childhood home. Her husband's family, however, ate rice at mealtime. As a member of an intercultural family she has learned to eat rice regularly for dinner, and potatoes are served only once or twice each month. Someone had to give in.

Whereas many couples can adapt quite easily to dietary changes, that may not always be feasible or desirable. A mutually agreeable arrangement may take time and negotiation, but eating habits are an important part of living together.

MORAL GUIDELINES

In Fred's family behavioral codes were clearly stated, not only by his parents but in pledges he had to sign at his Christian schools. Anita's background was governed more by moral principles than by specific lists of acceptable activities.

Although spouses are no longer under direct parental authority, they will continue to be guided by parental influences. Morality is not an easily negotiated area of life. Right and wrong may be absolute in some cultures but situational in others.

TRADITIONS

Family and cultural tradition can be viewed from different perspectives: as a way of life or a flexible framework for celebrations and activities. For instance, when some couples marry one or both of the spouses may expect to continue the traditions he or she grew up with. Activities such as spending Sunday afternoons with the parents and celebrating holidays can be especially difficult for a spouse who feels forced to conform to the other's patterns. Although some tensions regarding traditions can be worked out after the wedding, many issues need to be resolved prior to marriage.

CONFLICT RESOLUTION

In some cultures people are more expressive of their feelings than in others. When something is wrong, they are willing to let their spouse know how they feel immediately. But other cultures tend to avoid confrontation. A spouse from such a background may internalize emotions.

Many people communicate better nonverbally than they do verbally. Although it is impossible to read a person's mind, it is important to learn to interpret actions, reactions, and voice tones accurately.

RED LIGHTS

Should couples ever be advised *against* interracial or intercultural marriage?

First of all, there are legal reasons people should not marry (even someone within their own race or culture). These may include being under age; marriage to a parent, sibling, or close cousin; government restrictions; or police probation. As recently as thirty years ago, twenty-five states had antimiscegenation laws prohibiting interracial marriage.

Are there social and cultural deterrents to intermarriage as well? We believe there are five red lights that should cause couples to delay, postpone, or cancel plans to marry. These lights are not necessarily permanent obstacles, erected in concrete. They are basic reasons couples should not proceed at the present time.

IMPROPER MOTIVATIONS

Several years ago a couple came to Fred, asking him to perform their wedding ceremony. The two had had a brief affair, and the woman was pregnant. The man felt obligated to accept responsibility for the mother and the expected child. As they discussed their various options, Fred asked the man if he loved the woman.

"Not really," he answered.

Then Fred turned to the woman and asked her the same question.

"I don't think so," she replied.

Fred refused to marry the couple, not because the woman was pregnant, but because they did not love each other.

In a previous chapter, we examined various motivations that may cause a person to marry interracially or interculturally. If hostility, revenge, idealism, or rebellion is the reason for intermarriage, that should be a warning signal to all concerned. Do not proceed!

DISAGREEMENT CONCERNING CULTURAL IDENTITY

With which culture (or race) will the couple identify after marriage? Will they try to identify with both cultures or neither? Experts differ widely as to the best approach. Whereas it is not essential that partners agree with the opinions of other people, it is foundational that they agree between themselves.

Some believe it is important to identify with the dominant culture in a community. Others think that for the children's sake families should identify with the minority community. Still others state that interracial couples should not marry at all because they won't be accepted by either culture.

In many wedding ceremonies the bride and the groom light a large candle called "the unity candle." Together the partners light the candle with their individual candles, then the bride and groom extinguish their individual candles, symbolizing that the two have become one. When we were married in 1955, that symbolic act usually meant that the wife gave up her maiden name, aspirations, and uniqueness to identify completely with her husband.

Because the two were to become one, it was considered essential to find a partner as much like you as possible—someone with whom you had grown up, played, and gone to school. An ideal spouse shared your economic background, religious views, and ethnic and racial heritage. In order to literally "become one," the couple needed to have as much in common as possible. When choosing a mate, people looked for their "kind of person."

Because society was less mobile then, it was easier to find someone with a similar background. Even then, however, young people often discovered that opposites attract, in spite of their parents' wishes. The likelihood of a spouse being "different" greatly increased as young people went off to war, attended schools away from home, or found jobs in other cities.

Was the phrase "becoming one" synonymous with losing one's own identity? How did it relate to the symbolism of the unity candle? Couples began to reconsider that ceremony. They still lighted the unity candle with their individual candles, but they no longer extinguished their own lights. Becoming one no longer meant abandoning one's uniqueness and identity.

DIFFERENCES IN RELIGIOUS BELIEFS

Whether the couple be Christian, Buddhist, Hindu, Jew, Muslim, agnostic, or atheist, religion is a universal issue that must be addressed before marriage. The partners may consider religious belief merely a preference or a secondary matter. However, when one or both of the individuals is strongly committed to his or her faith, religion is no longer a negotiable item.

The apostle Paul exhorts Christians, "Do not unite yourselves with unbelievers; they are no fit mates for you" (2 Corinthians 6:14, NEB*). When addressing the subject of remarriage, Paul gives widows the same ad-

*New English Bible.

vice: "If the husband dies, she is free to marry whom she will, provided the marriage is within the Lord's fellowship" (1 Corinthians 7:39, NEB).

We agree with the popular evangelical Christian position on interfaith and interracial marriage stated by James Daane in *Dictionary of Christian Ethics:*

> Scripture makes only one stipulation about any Christian's marriage. Man is required to marry "in the Lord." The Scriptures do not limit a Christian's right to marry a Christian of another race or color. Consequently, no state or human society, or church has the Biblical right to forbid interracial marriages.[3]

In a survey of twenty-five white Baptist ministers who indicated that they approved of intermarriages between believing Christians but not interfaith marriages, one pastor expressed his position thus: "God draws distinction between Christians and non-Christians, but He does not recognize race."[4] This is a biblical position, not a denominational one.

UNDERGROUND NATURE OF THE RELATIONSHIP

Dating often becomes a game between parents and children. Parents are perceived as trying to get as much information as they can, and children are perceived as trying to conceal everything. Whereas those perceptions may be accurate in any dating relationship, the clandestine scenario is intensified when the dating falls into the interracial/intercultural category. Simply because of the stigma society attaches to interracial dating and marriage, many relationships begin in an unwholesome environment.

It is healthy and normal to have friends who do not belong to one's own family, close circle, or culture. Yet parents can tell when casual friendships develop into something more serious. Teenagers don't need to tell their parents everything about their personal lives, but they do need to prove themselves trustworthy. Denying the nature of the dating relationship strains the dynamics between parents and children and often leads to further deception.

Oliver Petrovich, aged twenty-three, was charged with two accounts of second-degree murder after killing his parents with a shotgun. Petrovich shot his parents after they discovered that he'd hidden his nineteen-year-old black girlfriend in their home. He'd hidden her in his room, closets, the car, and the garage. Oliver's father, of Yugoslavian descent, became enraged when the secret was discovered. After he ordered the girlfriend out of the house, Oliver took a shotgun and murdered his parents.[5]

Few interracial couples would go to that extreme to deceive their parents, but many do decide that the only way their relationship can survive is to go underground. Janet Bode, author of *Different Worlds*, warns couples not to go underground. "Don't continue to see each other in secret. 'Why not?' Because the main focus of your time together is sneaking around. Instead of going out and having fun, you're busy plotting and lying."[6]

Lynn E. Ponton, a psychiatrist who works with adolescents at the University of California Medical Center in San Francisco, routinely sees patients who are involved in interracial and cross-cultural dating. She underscores the problems that often result from a concealed relationship. "If the couple takes the relationship underground, in some ways it can become very romantic: us against the world. What you lose, though, is the chance to experience the ordinary ups and downs of dating. Each contact has to be secretive. You have to go through all sorts of planning to get together. That spicy edge becomes exciting and may even be what binds you together.[7]

PARENTAL DISAPPROVAL

The Bible is quite clear that children should obey their parents. Is that injunction an indefinite one? When is an individual no longer considered a child? At age eighteen? twenty-one? when he or she moves out of the house?

Being born into a family positions one in a lifetime relationship. We will always be children of our parents and parents of our children. The family is a God-ordained institution. When children leave home they are no longer under the direct authority of their parents, but they should continue to seek their advice and counsel.

Although all rules regarding dating seem reasonable to parents, they may appear inconsistent and stupid to teenagers. Parents' rules may restrict when teenagers are allowed to date, the age of people they can date, where they can go, how often they can go out, curfew limits, and so on. Parents also make judgments about the types of individuals their teenagers date. Although often subjective in nature, their decisions are usually based on experience and intuition.

Social and cultural prejudice—whether subtle or overt—affects parental restrictions. Teenagers can be blinded to other issues when they want to date someone of another race or culture. In an interview with *Interrace* magazine, Janet Bode cautions teenagers not to focus on a single issue such as race when discussing a parent's reasons for prohibiting them from dating. "If the person you are seeing is addicted to drugs, involved with the law, in multiple relationships, and has a lot of other things involved with his or her character, maybe you're pretending that your parents are saying it's a racial thing, when in reality the guy's a real scum-bag."[8]

When a parent does not approve of or accept a potential spouse, that becomes a red light. The reasons for disapproval may be prejudice or racism. On the other hand, the reasons may have nothing to do with race. No matter what the grounds, sufficient opportunity needs to be given for the parents and potential spouse to get acquainted and approve of the decision. And that takes time.

Every couple—especially interracial couples— needs the support of the significant people in their lives. Although they may no longer live with their parents, it is wise to listen to their counsel. We have talked to many couples who were thankful they had listened to their parents' advice. Some even postponed or canceled their plans to marry. Extra time spent developing relationships before marriage is well worth the effort.

No matter how negative one's parents may be about interracial and intercultural dating, disobeying their rules and disregarding their authority will not in the long run (or even the short run) develop a healthy atmosphere for the relationship.

Denial, deception, and disobedience affect everyone. In order to change stereotypes and prejudices as well as understand parents' wisdom and insights, everyone must be willing to work hard to develop a climate of open and honest communication. Parents have a responsibility to initiate these discussions prior to the dating period. However, once an interracial dating relationship has begun, it is up to the son or daughter to facilitate discussion and find ways to prevent heated confrontation.

When teenagers are willing to discuss their friendships and experiences with their parents, race and ethnic heritage may never become the main focus of discussion. Talking about other issues, such as familiarity between both sets of parents and both neighborhoods, the friend's religious background, age, values, friends, and so on will help lessen the possibility that skin color and diversity of culture become the overriding issues.[9]

Young people should try to let their parents become acquainted with their friends in neutral or nonthreatening environments before interracial dating becomes a confrontational issue. Tensions lessen when the boyfriend or girlfriend is not a complete stranger. Children can invite parents to social or athletic events, open houses, or birthday parties where parents can observe and talk to their friends. A child might also suggest that his or her parents speak to a mutual acquaintance about the friend—a teacher, coach, librarian, guidance counselor, neighbor, store owner, or employer.[10] When parents can receive input from people whose opinions and judgments they respect, the relationship with their child will go more smoothly.

GREEN LIGHTS

In addition to the warning lights, it is good to recognize green lights in dating relationships. No one can always predict the success or failure of a marriage, but some signs tend to indicate that it is OK to proceed.

INTERNAL STABILITY

When individuals feel good about themselves, they are more likely to have a healthy marriage. It is easier to love a partner who is different from you when that partner loves himself or herself. Couples should have open minds; each partner should understand his or her own feelings and motives. Ultimately, however, marriage is a decision of the will. Based on one's intellect and emotions, a commitment is made to another person for "as long as we both shall live." Marriage that is viewed as an experiment or as a trial for "as long as we both shall love" is doomed from the beginning. Lifetime commitments require inner strength from God to succeed.

EXTERNAL SUPPORT

Before a wedding ceremony, someone will occasionally say, "Tie a good knot." Fred's response is always the same: "I'm not the one who ties the knot." God does that, and He uses three strands. One strand represents the groom, and the second strand represents the bride. The third strand is the significant people in the couple's lives who will form their support system. If family, relatives, friends, and associates accept and approve of the marriage, the possibility of a lasting relationship is enhanced. Continual affirmation becomes a foundation of stability necessary to a successful marriage.

SPIRITUAL STRENGTH

Although a legal transaction, marriage is more than the possession of a civil document authorizing a couple to be married. It is the union of two individuals who need spiritual strength above and beyond what internal and external support systems can provide. The act of marriage, ordained by God, needs to be maintained on a spiritual level. The phrase "families that pray together, stay together" is much more than a cute or catchy slogan. It is an important truth.

Interracial and intercultural marriages require more strength than marriages between couples with similar backgrounds. All marriages experience pressure within, but pressure exerted from outside the marriage puts an even greater strain on those who intermarry.

In the United States any couple can journey from singlehood to marriage with little or no regard for any of the aforementioned traffic lights. Some who intentionally disregard the caution lights may have long-lasting and happy marriages, but many will not. Like wearing seat belts, obeying these lights does not eliminate fatalities. Paying attention to them doesn't guarantee success, but it does reduce the risk of heartache.

Before entering into an interracial relationship, differences should first be discussed with a counselor who understands racial and cultural distinctions. It can be deceiving, possibly disastrous, to go through premarital counseling without discussing these differences.

NOTES

1. Francislee Osseo-Asare, *A New Land to Live In* (Downers Grove, Ill.: Inter-Varsity, 1977), p. 9.
2. Ernest Porterfield, *Black and White Mixed Marriages* (Chicago: Nelson-Hall, 1978), p. 11.
3. *Baker Dictionary of Christian Ethics*, s.v. "intermarriage."
4. Paul R. Spickard, *Mixed Blood: Intermarriage and Ethnic Identity in Twentieth-Century America* (Madison: U. of Wisconsin, 1989), p. 364.
5. "White Man Kills Parents Over Black Girlfriend," *Jet* (October 17, 1988): 54.
6. Janet Bode, *Different Worlds: Interracial and Cross-Cultural Dating* (New York: Franklin Watts, 1989), p. 56.
7. Ibid.
8. "Talking To . . . " *Interrace* (March/April 1990): 38.
9. Bode, *Different Worlds*, p. 91.
10. Ibid., pp. 60-61.

6

MIXED UP
Lock Your Doors

We both grew up in suburban Chicago. Living in the shadow of a large city influenced our views of the world. We lived in anticipation of occasional trips to the "Windy City" to shop, visit relatives, or go to museums and other attractions. For several weeks prior to such excursions we'd save our money and dream about how we'd spend it.

Our parents made sure, however, that we understood that Chicago was no fairyland or Santa's Village. The big, bad city contained people who couldn't be trusted. Just as we heard that all the people who lived in the country were "bumpkins," we were told that all the people who lived in the city (except our relatives, of course) were "city slickers."

Whether we took the train into Chicago or arrived by car, our world suddenly changed the moment we crossed the city limits. Chicago's mystique contributed both to our fear and to our fascination with the strange world we called "the city."

Fred's folks usually traveled to Chicago by train, whereas Anita's family came by car from nearby Indiana, approaching through the south side of Chicago. As soon as her family entered a black neighborhood, An-

75

ita's father would turn around and holler, "Lock your doors!"

Parents usually lock car doors to keep their children from falling out, but in the city doors are locked to keep criminals from getting in. "If you don't protect yourself, you're crazy," we'd both been warned. "'Cause those niggers will rob you of everything you've got." These negative remarks left deep impressions on our young minds. Not only were black people different; they were dangerous.

Fred's parents, second generation European-Americans, had no friends of African, Asian, or South American ancestry. Even though all of their friends from church and the neighborhood were of European descent, his parents did not consider themselves prejudiced. After all, many of his relatives labored as missionaries to the heathen in Zaire when it was called the Belgian Congo. Countless hours and considerable energy were spent shipping supplies to Africa and sending prayer letters to donors and prayer warriors across the United States. Love for Africa's heathen motivated the family's efforts.

It was a "safe" love, however. It's easy to love from a distance. If any of those heathen had moved to the United States after conversion, they would not have been welcome in Fred's parents' home, neighborhood, or church. His mother once voiced one of her greatest fears to Anita, confiding, "I hope Fred doesn't bring any of his black friends home from college."

In the 1950s Fred's dad worked as a foreman at a Chicago printing firm. His only contact with minorities was from a position of power as their boss. On one occasion he had to decide which of the black women he supervised would be transferred to another department. He had all the women form a line. Then without thinking, he began to recite the children's rhyme "Eenie, meenie, minie, moe, catch a nigger by the toe." Although he realized the offense once he'd begun, he didn't pause or apologize. Instead, he continued to the end of the rhyme. It would have been unacceptable for Fred's parents to have friends of another race and unthinkable for their children to consider intermarriage.

Anita's parents, on the other hand, were more willing to discuss their racial prejudices. Her father's ancestry was Irish. In spite of the fact that some Irish immigrants had suffered persecution in the United States, Anita's father felt superior to most people of different ethnic and racial origins. He called every group by its derogatory label, especially those with different skin colors. Whenever Anita brought friends home, her father wanted to know their nation of origin. The only group he approved of other than the Irish were the English because his wife's ancestors had come to America from England in 1629.

Anita's mother, a kind, gentle, Southern woman, did not think of herself as prejudiced. After all, she had loved her Negro mammy as a child. "I don't have anything against Negroes," she would say when challenged about her views. But when asked if her mammy had ever been invited to eat in the family dining room, she would justify her answer, saying, "It just wasn't done." Growing up in Kentucky in the early part of the twentieth century, Anita's mother had been taught that whites and blacks each had their own place. That meant separate churches, schools, drinking fountains, and train seats. Although her ancestors had owned slaves, Anita's mother would always explain that "they were kind to their people and treated them far better than most."

Because neither of us had much personal contact with people of other races and cultures while we were young, it became convenient to categorize them indiscriminately. With our parents' and peers' support, we gave every group a descriptive label. Those labels and stereotypes became part of our belief system.

Before we discuss how to support interracial families, we need to consider the two powerful forces that shape our thinking, attitudes, and beliefs: stereotyping and racism. A stereotype is a mental picture or a standard opinion of a person, group, issue, or event. Although the less dangerous of the two, stereotyping contains the destructive seeds of racism. People who are objects of stereotyping are viewed as conforming to unvarying patterns without exception.

Stereotypes usually originate from two sources. We learn attitudes from our family environment or cultural background. And we create stereotypes from isolated personal encounters with individuals of other groups.[1]

Stereotyping is not always good or bad. It helps us to deal with an abundance of information in our complex environment, providing an easier way to categorize people and events. An example from our past illustrates how the two of us dealt with a stereotype about weather.

When we moved to Oregon, we discovered that we each held a stereotype about rain. We enjoyed the people and the scenery, but Oregon's climate had a negative impact on us. It rained nearly every day throughout our first winter in Portland.

We had come from "snow country," where we thought of snow as beautiful, clean, refreshing, lovely, and white. Rain, on the other hand, seemed dreary, miserable, and depressing.

Our stereotype of rain changed after about a year in Oregon. In order for our mind-sets to be altered, however, it was necessary for us to be exposed to the benefits of rain. Had we not lived in Oregon, we probably would still dislike rain.

Stereotyping the weather does little damage, but when negative labels are attached to entire groups of people, it can be devastating. Groups have been categorized according to physical features, size, and skin pigmentation.

Dr. Mary Jo Nolin, a Washington, D.C., sociologist, describes how the process works: "You see people for the first time, you relate to them on the basis of their sex, whether they're male or female, their visual clues as to their age, their race, and their culture. In other words, when you come to an encounter with a stranger, you already have certain expectations that give you a structure in which to deal with each other, and that works fine in those situations where all you need to know is the person's role."[2]

An African-American pastor once explained how black people think whites categorize other races: "If you're yellow, you're mellow; if you're brown, stick around; if you're black, get back; and if you're white, you're all right." In a *Sports Illustrated* article, Reggie Jackson said, "It seems the darker a person's complexion, the more fear he produces in other people. I'm not sure why that is, but people darker than I am can sense the fear."[3]

The easiest people to stereotype are those with identifiable characteristics. People of color are usually subject to the greatest degree of negative stereotyping. For example, think about the ways we distinguish between black and white in everyday conversation, and consider how we transfer those descriptions to people groups. Many of the images connected with the word *black* are negative—dirty, filthy, foul, nasty, soiled, unclean. If you want to smear someone, you blacken his name. "Black market," "black eye," "blackout," "blacklist," "blackmail," "black mark," "black sheep," and "blackball" all have negative connotations.

On the other hand, think about how the word *white* is used in our society. Such definitions as innocent, clean, and pure come to mind. A "white lie" isn't as bad as other lies. To "whitewash" someone is to acquit him or her of any wrongdoing.

One way to describe people is by color—of their hair, eyes, or skin. In Darwin Walton's book for children, *What Color Are You?* the author comments,

> Color and many shades of color help make life more interesting and enjoyable. Color makes the identification of people and things easier. Wouldn't it be dull if all the houses were painted the same shade of yellow, or weren't painted at all? Try imagining all of the people you knew having the same color of eyes, hair, and skin. That wouldn't be at all exciting. When you meet a new friend, it's much easier to describe him in terms of skin, hair, and eye color. It wouldn't be quite so easy to speak of him only in terms of his size and shape.[4]

When color is used to describe a house, it reflects individual taste and preference. When color is used symbolically to describe groups of people, it has a completely different meaning. Color symbolism is one of the seeds of racism in our society.

When we were children in Sunday school, we were both introduced to *The Wordless Book*. Each page of the book was a different color—black, red, white, gold, and green. The book had no words, only five colored pages. The colors were a simple but profound way to explain the process of salvation to children. Gold represented heaven; green stood for growth; red depicted blood. Guess which color represented sin and evil? Which color do you suppose stood for purity and goodness? It was not the intent of that book to make stereotypes. Unconsciously, however, we began to identify the color white with right and the color black with wrong. Because neither of us had any friends whose pigmentation was different from ours, the stereotypes remained. We now wonder how black boys and girls felt when they heard the explanation of *The Wordless Book.*

Barbara McIntyre, editor of an interracial catalog, describes color symbolism as

> a language in which colors are used to represent concepts that have nothing to do with the colors themselves. When a color becomes a symbol, it is no longer just a visual experience. Instead, color evokes an emotional response, which will likely be expressed below one's level of awareness. Although the way these ideas are usually presented is very subtle, the concept is strong and destructive.[5]

Our daughter-in-law, Martha, and son-in-law, Bruce, are like each other in skin color, but their similarity ends there. They differ from each other in almost every other way. The elementary school in the small Louisiana town where Martha was raised did not fully integrate black and white students until 1989, thirty-five years after *Brown vs. Board of Education I & II of Topeka, Kansas,* in which the Supreme Court declared "separate but equal" facilities in public schools unconstitutional. Unfortunately, the 1954 ruling that school segregation must be ended "with all deliberate speed" was not put into practice with the same sense of urgency in all areas of the United States.

Bruce, on the other hand, grew up in the state of New York where segregation was less overt and equal education more readily available. Experiences at the university level widened his opportunities even further. We became aware of inconsistencies in our own thinking as we got to know both of them and the differences in their upbringing. By stereotyping all black people as being alike, we distorted the variables between racial and cultural differences.

People use stereotypes to refer to both color and culture, which are sometimes viewed synonymously. In today's society, however, they need to be distinguished. When we are born into this world, we have a certain skin color and we enter into a certain culture. Although we can change our culture or adapt to it, our skin color is a different matter; it cannot be changed. These characteristics—color and culture—remain powerful forces in American society.

In a speech titled "With Culture, but Without Color," Dr. James Earl Massey, dean of Anderson Graduate School of Theology, said,

> Make no mistake about it, color and culture have meaning. We must neither de-emphasize color nor idolize it. God must have posited some meaning in what color brings into the human picture, since every human being has some color.
>
> Color is a tangible factor of personhood; it is related to a human being and is therefore a part of that person's total human factor. Color is not negotiable. It is a fact of nature for which no one ought to have to apologize or feel lacking. Because it is also a community property, i.e., a distinctive that appertains to a vast aggregate of persons, color is one of the universal factors of meaning in human life.
>
> Cultures, however, are negotiable and arbitrary. They are localized and historically oriented, and not God derived anthropological givens. Color is an anthropological fact, while culture is a human development.[6]

Since we are part of a cultural system that unfortunately produces racial stereotypes, we should make every possible effort to reverse the negative images, labels, and categories we have learned. Stereotypes may produce prejudice, discrimination, and racism. Unless they are exposed and changed, they will continue to be passed from generation to generation.

By the time our granddaughter Marquita, a child of black/white parents, entered school, she already knew that the tint of her skin was different from either of her parents. When she drew pictures of her family, she would color her father white, her mother black, and herself brown. Although she recognized differences of light and dark, she placed no judgment on the significance of these differences. They did not imply superiority or inferiority, beauty or ugliness.

We visited Marquita shortly before she entered second grade, and we noticed that she also associated skin color with traits and preferences. When our family went out to dinner one evening, all of us except Marquita's mother, Martha, ordered pizza.

"Black people don't like pizza," Marquita commented when her mother ordered another item from the menu.

"What did you say?" Martha asked her.

"Black people don't like pizza," she responded, realizing from her mother's tone of voice that she must have said something wrong.

When asked why she would make such a statement, Marquita explained that her uncle, her aunt, and her mother didn't like pizza, all three of whom are black. From Marquita's limited perspective, she jumped from individual preferences to a general categorization. It doesn't take children long to move from distinguishing outward differences in people to associating inward qualities with entire ethnic groups.

Our perception of beauty has a profound affect on our view of equality. If a people group is assigned an inferior position because of physical characteristics, their inequality in society is inevitable. Fortunately (or unfortunately), beauty is in the eye of the beholder. Stereotypes affect our standards of beauty. For many people the saying "Beauty is only skin deep" is all too true. The problem is that the standards have been set by the dominant race, which is still white in the United States. Blonde hair, blue eyes, and light skin remain the standard of beauty for many Americans. Unfortunately, that criteria has been imposed upon minority groups too.

In the 1940s Dr. Kenneth Clark and his wife, Mamie, tested schoolchildren regarding their view of beauty. They found that "two-thirds of the black children preferred white dolls to black dolls, and routinely saw black dolls as less beautiful and less intelligent. In a repeat of the Clark tests [in 1986] two-thirds of the black children still preferred white dolls."[7]

Colorism, rather than racism, is becoming a dominant theme in the world today, and one reason is the imprecise nature of race. A person's skin color is identifiable, whereas his race is often uncertain. South Africa, for instance, has a devastating system of classifying people by color. It is based on appearance, not anthropological criteria. Such features as complexion, hair type, speech, and palms of hands are closely examined. During 1989 more than twelve hundred people in South Africa applied to have their race changed. By administrative decisions "519 coloreds became white; two whites became Chinese; 59 Indians became colored; and 55 coloreds became Indians. Other decisions granted coloreds to change to Chinese, blacks to coloreds, and Malays to Indians. No blacks were changed into whites, and no whites became blacks."[8]

Discrimination based on racial or ethnic characteristics is illegal in the United States. Congress passes laws that guarantee protection in the marketplace and classroom, and to some extent behavior can be modified. But racism still exists because laws cannot force equality. Equality is more than accepting a person legally, biologically, or culturally. There must also be a willingness to accept him or her as an equal member of the human race.

Confusion continues as the world attempts to categorize racial and ethnic groups. National, state, and provincial governments struggle with how to differentiate without allowing the categories to become a basis for discrimination. People are divided into groups for gathering statistical data, allocating governmental funding, or establishing quotas, rather than for scientific or anthropological purposes.

The Michigan Department of Education has divided racial and ethnic groups into five categories:

1. *American Indian and Alaskan Native*—a person having origins in any of the original peoples of North America or who maintains cultural identification through tribal affiliation or community recognition.

2. *White, not of Hispanic Origin*—a person having origins in any of the original peoples of Europe, North Africa, or the Middle East.

3. *Black, not of Hispanic Origin*—a person having origins in any of the black racial groups of Africa.

4. *Asian or Pacific Islander*—a person having origins in any of the original peoples of the Pacific Islands. This area includes, for example, China, Japan, Korea, the Philippine Islands, and Samoa.

5. *Hispanic*—a person of Mexican, Puerto Rican, Cuban, Central or South American, or other Spanish culture or origin, regardless of race.[9]

Differences between categories are not always clear and precise. Placement in a category should not cause discrimination against a person. In incidences of intermarriage, persons should have the freedom to identify with whatever category or categories they choose.

Those who intermarry find themselves victims of discrimination because they cannot be easily categorized in many classification systems. Census forms and questionnaires have no category for biracial and multiracial families.

Because intermarried families are few in number, it is easy for stereotypes to arise. Before we can respond positively to interracial families, we need to recognize that many myths have developed about them. The following stereotypes, or myths, have been compiled from a number of sources, including conversations and observations:

1. Interracial marriage is contrary to biblical example and teaching.
2. Interracial partners are maladjusted and neurotic.
3. Only white people question the advisability of interracial marriage.
4. Interracial couples have a higher divorce rate than couples of the same race.
5. Biracial children will be rejected by both races.
6. Interracial offspring have weaker genes.
7. Interracial children are victims of parents' choices.

Stereotypes need to be examined for their validity. Removing negative stereotypes, however, is not simply an intellectual exercise. Most people don't change their views until they are exposed firsthand to interracial families who lead harmonious lives.

Just as we had to move to Oregon to change our stereotypes of rain, so we need to interact socially with interracial families to change our stereotypes of people. Stereotypes develop in an environment where everything is the same. Negative stereotyping begins to crumble when people are exposed to different individuals. Respect and trust cannot be developed from a distance.

The Christian as beholder is to be color-blind, not because varieties of color cannot be appreciated but because they should not determine who is the "fairest of them all."

"When I was a child, I talked like a child, I thought like a child, I reasoned like a child. When I became a man, I put childish ways behind me. Now we see but a poor reflection as in a mirror" (1 Corinthians 13:11-12). There will always be inequality, as long as mirrors reflect human standards. God's standard, however, is that all people are created equal. Pamela Frankau observes that "there must come a time when . . . all your mirrors turn into windows."[10] For the Christian the window is Jesus Christ.

What's a Man Worth?

What's a man worth?
Does anyone know?
Is he measured by riches,
By friend or by foe?

Can we tell by his virtues,
His station of life?
His accent? His color?
His people, or his strife?

The length of his hair?
The shape of his nose,
His smile or his handshake,
The cut of his clothes?

What's a man worth?
We turn to our guide,
and Christ gives the answer
"For each man I died."

(Anonymous)[11]

NOTES

1. Sterling Stucky, *Slave Culture* (New York: Oxford, 1987), p. 36.

2. Janet Bode, *Different Worlds: Interracial and Cross-Cultural Dating* (New York: Franklin Watts, 1989), p. 36.

3. Reggie Jackson, "We Have a Serious Problem That Isn't Going Away," *Sports Illustrated* (May 11, 1987): 41.

4. Darwin Walton, *What Color Are You?* (Chicago: Johnson, 1973), pp. 28-29.

5. Barbara McIntyre, "Who's the Fairest of Them All," *People of Every Stripe* [catalog] (Winter 1989): 8.

6. James Earl Massey. "With Culture but Without Color." Seminar on the theology of evangelism presented at the American Festival of Evangelism, Kansas City, Missouri, July 28, 1981.

7. Juan Williams, "The Color of Their Skin," *Parenting* (March 1988): 51.

8. Howard Witt, "Tinted by Law," *Chicago Tribune*, Sunday, May 27, 1990, Tempo section.

9. Michigan Department of Education, *Race and Ethnic Standards for Federal Statistics and Administrative Reporting*, Directive no. 15.

10. B. J. Chute, "When the Writer Comes of Age," in *The Writer's Handbook*, ed. A. S. Burack (Boston: The Writer, 1975), p. 34.

11. Quoted in Dick Brogan, comp., *Not Our Kind of Folks?* (Nashville: Broadman, 1978), p. 46.

7

MIXED REVIEWS
With(in) or Without

Our family has moved many times. When we are in the process of relocating, people often ask, "Do you know what you're getting into?" Our answer is usually, "No. If we knew what we were getting into, we probably wouldn't do anything." It might be nice to be able to look into the future occasionally, but uncertainty can be a blessing as well.

Racial issues were far from our minds as we faced the 1980s. We never would have predicted that the subject of interracial marriage would become a dominant theme in our lives. Our concern for our children centered on school and church activities and lifestyle choices.

If racial issues did exist, they were someone else's problem. Civil rights were guaranteed by law. Riots, looting, and burnings were of the past. Neighborhoods were mixed, schools were integrated, and athletic teams were made up of players of every color of the rainbow. Neither the negative nor the positive aspects of racial changes had affected us personally. Although we had nonwhite acquaintances, none of our closest friends belonged to any other race.

We were totally unprepared for the unique ways our family would enter into the racial struggle. Our two older children married black people. We are now grandparents of two biracial children. As we near the end of this millennium, we look back at the drastic changes that have occurred in our perspective.

National attention shifts from the economy to global warfare, but the issues of racism and prejudice continue to rear their ugly heads. Hatred and bigotry are still in the forefront internationally, nationally, and locally.

The front page of a recent edition of Portland's daily newspaper contained a variety of headlines. "1500 Rally Against Prejudice" described a peaceful march in memory of an Ethiopian man who was beaten to death by skinheads. A second headline on the same page read, "Interracial Couple Receives Threats." Their crime? Being interracially married. On the same page was "David Duke Stronger Than Ever." Duke, a former Ku Klux Klansman who was running for the Senate in Louisiana, was to draw 44 percent of the total votes and nearly 60 percent of the white vote in the election that followed.

The color issue is still a reality. Racial lines remain more difficult to cross than economic, educational, national, or religious lines.

The problem of racism is complex; it cannot be eradicated by education or laws. It is a disease of the heart, and laws are not written on the heart. Although the specific focus of this book is interracial and intercultural marriage, it is difficult to separate this topic from racism.

Few people will admit to being racist. It's easy to assign racism to "back there" in history or to some place "out there" in the rest of the world.

Some people deny that they are racist, explaining that there just isn't anyone of a different race in their community, school, or church. Others will deny they are racist by saying, "Some of my best friends are niggers," or, "I played basketball with blacks in high school," or, "We have foreigners who work in my office [factory, shop]."

PREJUDICE

Prejudice is different from racism. The literal meaning of the word *prejudice* is to "prejudge." It has been described as "being down on what you are not up on." In his classic book *The Nature of Prejudice*, Gordon Allport says, "Prejudice is an antipathy based upon a faulty and inflexible generalization. It may be felt or expressed. It may be directed toward a group as a whole or toward an individual because he is a member of that group."[1] Prejudices are based upon myths, stereotypes, and traditions—seldom upon facts.

Pride in one's race or heritage has many positive aspects, but it may also lead to a sense of superiority, or prejudice, toward other people. Opinions and assumptions lead to prejudice when they are based on outward appearance, hearsay, or incorrect information.

All of us are prejudiced to some degree. It is always difficult to refrain from making judgments, but sometimes the information we base our judgments on is erroneous or insufficient. Most of us are willing to alter our misconceptions when we receive correct information. Yet when racial prejudice continues, despite all evidence to the contrary, it becomes racism.

RACISM

Racism, an extreme form of prejudice, cannot be eliminated by education or reason. Prejudice may be conscious or unconscious, but racism is a deliberate attempt to justify one's own racial superiority by assigning inferior qualities to other groups. Racists explain differences genetically, rather than environmentally.

Perhaps our discussion of racism would benefit from a comparative illustration. There are many similarities between racism and onions. Onions have little odor as long as they remain fresh and in the pantry. Similarly, as long as we have no contact with racism, we are not affected by it. But when the skin of the onion is peeled away, its pungent odor permeates the air. Whether we simply handle an onion or actually eat it, we cannot ignore the smell.

Once we slice an onion, we discover that the round, edible bulb consists of several concentric, easily separable layers. As with racism, it's not possible to get to the core without cutting through each layer. It is conceivable to handle the subject of racism by not touching it, treating it like an onion on the pantry shelf. But unless we cut into its layers, we will never discover how complex and personal the problem is. As we cut into racism, we begin to realize that we can't escape its reek.

BIBLICAL LAYER

Of all the books ever written, the Bible is the chief treatise on the worth of the individual. Because the Bible teaches that each person is created in God's image and possesses an eternal soul, there is no room for racial superiority in Christian circles. Why, then, do so many people insist that their prejudice against interracial marriage is biblically based?

Many people can't or won't give any reason for this claim, except to say that the Bible is opposed to intermarriage. Others are more specific and point to such passages as Nehemiah 13:25, where Nehemiah commands the Israelites, "You are not to give your daughters in marriage to their sons, nor are you to take their daughters in marriage for your sons or for yourselves."

One former professor thoroughly examined biblical passages pertaining to the mixing of races and people in the Old Testament. He summarizes his study:

> Analysis of the laws and the practice of mixed marriage in ancient Israel leads to the conclusion that the Bible does not forbid or condemn marriages with other races or people, but only those marriages contracted with an idolater or unbeliever. It should be clear to all who come to the Word of God with an open mind that any racist interpretation of the Bible is unwarranted.[2]

"TWO SEED" THEORY

Others who use the Bible to justify their opposition to racial mixing base their views on a pre-Adamic creation. A group called the Lord's Covenant Church uses such verses as Genesis 1:11 to support their views. They interpret this passage, which describes the land bearing fruit from seed, "according to their various kinds," as referring to the purity and separateness of the white race.[3]

A man from Florida used the same type of reasoning when he wrote to us about interracial marriage. He quoted Deuteronomy 22:9: "Do not plant two kinds of seed in your vineyard; if you do, not only the crops you plant but also the fruit of the vineyard will be defiled."

Two biblical objections to the "two seed" theory are that the passages refer to seeds, not people and that the theory is based on a pre-Adamic creation. The Bible teaches that all mankind came from one human source. Any belief in a polygenistic theory of creation must be rejected.

One well-known Christian educator goes so far as to state, "The cry today is 'one world, one race, one church,' but it will be a corrupt and evil world, a mongrel race, and the church of the anti-Christ. Intermarriage of the races is a breakdown of the lines of separation which God has set up and, therefore, is rebellion against God."[4]

Whereas racist views based on Scripture may not be as overtly proclaimed today as in the past, they are still held by many professing Christians. A retired executive of a Minnesota corporation was recently discovered to have sent 100,000 anonymous letters to mixed couples over a period of fourteen years, denouncing interbreeding as satanic. The letters containing scriptural references expounded the theory that God created separate races and that "Satan is on a rampage to destroy God's races."[5]

NOAH'S CURSE

Genesis 9:18-27 is the main Scripture passage used to support opposition to interracial marriage. This passage is often referred to as the "curse passage" and is used by both Christians and non-Christians.

The Genesis reference takes place after the Flood. Noah had three sons who survived the Deluge. All of the earth's inhabitants came from this family, even as they originally descended from Adam. Ham, one of Noah's sons, looked upon his father's nakedness. When Noah "found out what his youngest son had done to him, he said, 'Cursed be Canaan! The lowest of slaves will he be to his brothers'" (vv. 24-25). At the same time Noah's other two sons, Shem and Japheth, were blessed.

Racists (and many others) consider Noah's three sons to be the beginning of the three primary races— black, yellow, and white. Because of the devastating implications of the racist interpretation of this curse, it is essential that we examine the full meaning and significance of this passage.

First, we need to realize that the curse was directed not at Ham but at his youngest son, Canaan. Were the Canaanites the beginning of what we now refer to as the black race? According to William F. Albright, noted biblical scholar, "The progeny of Canaan are recorded in Genesis 10:15-19. It is clear they are not inhabitants of Africa and were not considered as black-skinned by those of the ancient world."[6]

At best the curse should be viewed as a prophecy. Israel conquered the Canaanites, and they became slaves of the Israelites. Of all the races, the Canaanites would be most closely identified with Caucasians! Also, Noah—not God—uttered this curse after Ham had awakened him from drunkenness. There is no indication that anybody's skin or physical features were altered because of this curse.[7]

WHAT THE BIBLE SAYS

What *does* the Bible teach about interracial marriage? Scripture teaches that there is oneness and equality in God's creation. "The God who made the world and everything in it is the Lord of heaven and earth. . . . From one man He made every nation of men, that they should inhabit the whole earth; and he determined the times set for them and the exact places where they should live" (Acts 17:24, 26).

The prophet Malachi underscores the monogenistic origin of humankind when he asks his rhetorical questions: "Have we not all one Father? Did not one God create us?" (Malachi 2:10). Biblically speaking, there is no basis for belief in a pre-Adamic creation different from the one recorded in Genesis.

So far we have examined some biblical passages and theories that opponents to interracial marriage use to support their position. But are there any positive examples of interracial marriage in the Bible? In Numbers 12:1-6 Miriam and Aaron criticize Moses because he had a Cushite wife. Cush was the first son of Ham and the father of the southernmost people known to the Hebrews. God punished Miriam and Aaron because of their opposition.

Two other famous intermarriages were between an Israelite and Rahab (from Canaan) and between an Israelite and Ruth (from Moab). Some might argue that just because God's people married foreign women, it doesn't mean that He blessed their partnerships. It's interesting to observe, however, that both of these women's names appear in the listing of the ancestry of Jesus Christ in Matthew 1:5, thus assigning them a place of honor.

Why do some Christians use the Bible as a basis for racism? One reason people become ethnocentric in their worldview is the sin of pride. But the Bible clearly teaches that all people are created equal in God's sight. Another reason for racist attitudes is that people misunderstand God's choosing a nation and the election of individuals. These doctrines are not based on the superiority of people but on God's sovereignty and grace.

Misinterpretation of Scripture is probably the greatest cause for racist views defended by the Bible. It has been said that the Bible is the most misquoted source in all the world.

It is extremely important that Christians do not encourage, directly or indirectly, those who claim that the Bible supports racist teachings. Clear understanding, teaching, and discussion of the biblical layer of racism are foundational to the consideration of other layers.

HISTORICAL LAYER

Racism as we know it today is fairly recent, but its roots run deep. Ethnocentrism is the belief that the attitudes, priorities, and behaviors of one's own group are better than those of other ethnic groups. Ethnocentrism precedes racism, although the two ideas are connected. Humanity's tendency is to believe that "my family," "my group," and "my race" do things better than outsiders. The feeling of superiority breeds hatred.

Hatred began with Cain, who murdered his brother Abel. Since that first act of animosity, the history of humankind has been an unending saga of bitterness. Joseph and his brothers, Jacob and Esau, and Ishmael and Isaac are examples of that sinful pattern.

It didn't take long for personal hostility to invade families, groups, clans, and nations. History records continued examples of hatred among peoples. "The Jew had his Gentile; the Greek had his barbarian; the Roman had his non-Roman; the Crusaders had their infidel; the 15th century Roman Catholics had their heathens; the English had their Irish; the Lutherans had their Anabaptists; the Nazis had their non-Arayans."[8]

Western civilization dominated the world by subjugating peoples, races, and countries—sometimes in the name of Christianity or "for the good of the people." What began as crusades in the name of Christ eventually became colonialism without the spiritual justification.

Racism reached a high (or low) under the Nazi regime of Adolph Hitler in the twentieth century. Teaching that Germans were a "master race," Hitler attempted to eliminate all non-Aryan people. His belief in "the survival of the fittest" was largely accepted in Nazi Germany. Where was the Christian church of Germany at that time? Other than a few scattered voices, opposition to Hitler's views was not pronounced.

But what does that have to do with Christians in the United States? It is easy to blame the Christian church of Germany for its silence prior to and during World War II, but what about the Christian church in

America during the same time period? Although Nazism was strongly denounced as a despotic military power and evil regime, little opposition was expressed toward the Nazis' racist views. In fact, many Americans of Nordic descent believed that the Nazi theory of racial superiority was valid.

It is difficult to divide America's history into exact periods of racial and ethnic style, but suffice it to say racism has continued to divide individuals and groups throughout all four centuries of our country's history. For the first 250 years large groups of people suffered greatly under the hands of the white majority. Native Americans saw their lands and resources taken from them. African-Americans not only suffered personally under the institution of slavery, they endured the destruction of their family life. During that period, the majority of white churches allowed slavery to continue without protest. Their leaders used Scripture and the forum of the pulpit to justify slavery and intimidate slaves into accepting their position in life.

After the Civil War, slaves were freed from bondage by law, but they did not achieve equality with those in power. Segregation became the bitter substitute for slavery. Native Americans were segregated on reservations, and when many African-Americans went North during the industrial revolution, they found more segregation in the "ghetto."

Increased immigration, mainly from Europe, brought millions of newcomers to America. Although many groups of newly arrived Europeans suffered humiliation and discrimination, they were eventually assimilated into the American "melting pot." After three or four generations, many European immigrants had lost their sense of cultural and ethnic heritage. Dark-skinned Americans, mainly African-Americans, could not be assimilated into the American society as easily.

Racial prejudice and antimiscegenation laws made it virtually impossible for blacks to change their status.

Although individual Christians and scattered churches spoke out against the evils of segregation, worship services were described as the most segregated hour in American life. In the midst of racial unrest, the federal government, rather than churches, pioneered the end of segregation in the 1950s and 1960s. By and large, America's churches were not in the forefront of the struggle for racial equality.

In the past thirty-five years since the historic Supreme Court decision declaring an end to segregation in the schools, some progress has taken place, but it has been slow in coming. Justice Thurgood Marshall, at the time of the *Brown vs. Board of Education of Topeka* decision in 1954, predicted that "by 1961 all forms of segregation in the United States would be eliminated."[9] He was wrong.

Events throughout history have not necessarily altered racist attitudes. Inequality can be imposed by outside forces, whereas equality comes only from a change of attitude.

SOUTHERN LAYER

America expanded numerically during the first three centuries of its existence due to large-scale immigration from Europe. Millions of people came to America because of their desire to be free. In contrast, two large groups of people were added to the population against their wills. Native Americans, who lived here before the Europeans arrived, were not forced to serve as slaves but were thrust into an American value system that always stereotyped them as the "bad guys." Even today children seldom volunteer for the Indian's role when they play "cowboys and Indians."

The other large group originally came as "indentured servants" from Africa but soon found themselves to be totally enslaved. Slavery became a way of life early in this country's history and continued to be practiced in the South until the Emancipation Proclamation in 1863.

Many arguments were used to justify slavery: it helped savages become cultured; plantation life was an ideal way to live; Negroes weren't human, weren't fit for freedom, and didn't want freedom.[10]

Some slave owners used the Bible and Christianity to prove that slavery was morally acceptable. Although not all Christians were slaveholders and not all slaveholders were Christians, the institution of slavery was inseparably intertwined with American Christianity. In *Slavery, Segregation and Scripture*, J. Oliver Buswell states that slave owners taught that slavery was of divine origin. Slaveholders, citing examples in the Old Testament and instructions in the New Testament, supported their subjugation of slaves.[11]

Slaves were taught that slavery was in their best interests. As a result, evangelistic efforts could not upset the social or political system. When African-Americans were converted, they were not usually allowed to worship in the "white folks" church with their masters. Brotherhood did not mean equality.

As we slice more deeply into this layer of racism, it is easy to dissociate ourselves from that segment of our nation's history. But not all racists resided in the South, nor did all victims of racism live south of the Mason-Dixon line.

None of us chose to be born or raised in a particular area of the world or within a particular family environment. In today's global village, however, we cannot remove ourselves from the universal struggle by claiming to be victims of our environment. Racism is not linked to where we live but to who we are.

INSTITUTIONAL LAYER

Racism did not end with the signing of the Emancipation Proclamation. Slaves were freed, but they possessed neither property, prestige, nor power to compete with white citizens. The institutions of society—government, schools, churches, marriage, and neighborhoods —remained separate and unequal.

In many ways segregation was an extension of colonialism and slavery. Although slaves were freed, they had no access to the tools they needed to change their status in life.

One phenomenon that perpetuated the abstract evils of slavery was the migration of blacks to northern cities. Former slaves became victims of another form of repression. The industrial revolution provided them with employment, but it did not necessarily improve their standard of living.

During this period, many white homeowners and churches fled the cities to the suburbs. This mass exodus, or "white flight," was motivated by "white fright." Ghettos emerged within large cities, where minorities— particularly African-Americans—became slaves to another institutional system.

People of color increasingly gained access to facilities, but they were not admitted into the social structures. Races were forbidden to mix as segregation and antimiscegenation laws kept the races from intermarrying. Although segregation officially ended in 1964, sixteen states still had antimiscegenation laws until all such laws were overturned by the Supreme Court on June 12, 1967. Legal barriers and sanctions have been eliminated from the statutes, but social pressures continue to restrict marriages between couples of differing racial groups in the United States.

No one can deny that tremendous changes have transpired in race relations during the past generation. Unfortunately for many people, especially minorities, integration has not become the fulfillment of a dream but is still a living nightmare. Has integration failed? Yes and no. Some middle-class people have made colossal strides. But many minorities, particularly those who dwell in the ghetto and in poor rural areas, continue to struggle with an America that for them is still separate and very unequal.[12]

Certain sections of society became integrated soon after the legal decisions were made, whereas other areas only experienced limited integration. Historian E. Franklin Frazier distinguishes between the "secular" and "sacred" arenas of integration. Secular, or secondary, settings are impersonal relationships. Restaurants, buses, trains, parks, stores, and public meeting places became integrated within a relatively short time. On the other hand, the sacred, or primary, institutions, such as the family, clubs, associations, and churches, which are social and personal in nature, did not experience the same degree of integration.[13]

Christians usually belong to several institutions besides the church. Many professional, athletic, and trade associations are still racist today, despite the laws of the land. Although membership applications and policies are not explicitly discriminatory, many unwritten practices remain so. Christians need to be in the forefront to make all institutions free from racial and cultural exclusiveness.

ECCLESIASTICAL LAYER

Where was the church when those social and political changes occurred? Throughout America's racial struggle, only a minority spoke out against the evils of racism or advocated social change. However, to the credit of many churches, some new denominations were formed because of their opposition to slavery. Before the Civil War, most churches were viewed by the oppressed as supporters of slavery.

Even after the Civil War, the church remained largely silent. Instead of being a leader in the fight against racism, it became a reflector of the mood of society. Rather than being a societal thermostat of racism, it was only a thermometer.

At best, churches sent mixed messages. Official pronouncements, creeds, and resolutions gave lip service to brotherhood, but the church was not in the forefront of the racial struggle. Christianity became more concerned with issues of personal piety than the issue of social justice. Yet social concern and evangelism do not have to compete with each other; they are complementary. The church should be concerned with the evil in the hearts of people *and* the evil in the environment and society.

When Fred attended a citywide men's breakfast on the East Coast in the 1960s, the speaker claimed that "God did not come to take people out of the slums; He came to take slums out of people." When we are forced to take an either/or position, we dilute the biblical message. Churches are to be both light and salt in society. Unfortunately the church usually opts for being light rather than salt. When given a choice, we often choose love and peace instead of truth and justice.

"The uncomfortable but well-established fact is that there is more racial prejudice in the church than outside of it," writes James E. Dittes in *Bias and the Pious*. "Racial prejudice is more likely to be found among churchgoers than among people who are not churchgoers," he claims.[14] Author John Perkins strongly identifies the "evangelical church, with a few exceptions . . . as the greatest stronghold of racism in America today."[15]

Whether or not such accusations are extreme, there is no question that racism does exist in our churches. The church preaches a message of love and reconciliation, so American society will judge the church by its own standard and message. Unfortunately most churches are strongly linked to their traditions. Change is not only slow; it is viewed as an enemy.

Eliminating racism requires that we recognize its existence and be willing to change the attitudes and activities that perpetuate it. We used a questionnaire to gather information about churches and racism in which we asked pastors, "Is there racism in your church?" The overwhelming majority answered no. Explanations included such remarks as, "We have several people of different races in our church, and they get along fine," or, "We don't have any people of different races in our community or in our church." However, the number of people of various races present or for that matter, absent, is not the main determinant of whether there is racism in the church. Attendance is only one factor.

A church in an urban area surrounded by children of different races and ethnic groups decided to have vacation Bible school. Since the parents wanted to avoid potential problems between their children and the neighborhood children, they decided to keep the vacation Bible school a secret. Only children who attended the church were invited. Another church defined the boundaries of their canvassing program to exclude the adjacent black neighborhood.

When a young pastor and his wife were called to a rural church they thrilled at the opportunity to serve God. Since the pastor was blind, his wife drove him to church and his pastoral calls; a seeing-eye dog also assisted the pastor in carrying out his duties. Although the congregation had little difficulty accepting their blind pastor or his seeing-eye dog, they did not accept his adopted black child.

To the pastor, the boy was simply his child, someone whom he loved even though he had never seen his son with physical eyes. The congregation, however, was blinded by prejudice. When churches judge people solely on outward appearance, they differ little from the world.

We need to ask,

"Why don't people of other races attend our church?"

"Are attenders part of the membership roll and fellowship circle?"

"Are our outreach efforts in the neighborhood and around the world directed toward people who are different?"

"Does the missionary budget reflect support for people of other nationalities and races?"

"Do our schools welcome people of other races into our programs?"

"Are young people of different races and cultures free to socialize, date, and marry?"

The church has remained largely silent on this subject. When it has spoken, its messages have been mixed. Although the church has given token and theoretical support to interracial and intercultural marriage, many church families transmit different messages. In other words, has the church taken the initiative to create racial harmony, or has it contributed to the problem through unwritten policies and indifference?

Two facts should be made clear concerning church-based responses to interracial and intercultural marriage. First, opposition to interracial marriage is not always because people are racist, although that is often the reason. A person's prejudice may be the result of misinformation, stereotypes, traditions, or lack of exposure to people who are unlike him.

Second, acceptance of interracial and intercultural marriage will not eliminate racism. In fact, it is entirely possible to be married interracially and still be a racist, just as it is possible to be cautious about interracial marriage and not be racist.

Many people refer to the church as "they." Someone has said that the most misquoted source in all the world besides the Bible is "they." The church is not "they"; it is "we." When we who are part of the church take a stand against racism, Christian brotherhood will become a reality.

CULTURAL LAYER

No culture or ethnic group is immune to prejudice. In order to maintain a sense of identity, ethnic groups compare themselves to other groups. Ethnicity can lead to ethnocentrism, which may include religious, educational, mental, theological, social, occupational, sexual, cultural, or racial comparisons. People around the world believe that their way is best. Ethnocentrism eventually leads to racism if we yield to the temptation to elevate ourselves at the expense of others.

Although we live in a pluralistic society, most of us are not comfortable with diversity. All races are guilty of extremes in promoting their culture as superior. In order to avoid dilution or elimination of one's particular culture, some promote an inclusivist approach.

"Nationalism always contains the seeds of racism," says Alan Davies in *Infected Christianity.* "Christians must never be allowed to forget that the Christ in whom they believe is always against as well as for their particular cultures."[16]

Christians need not deny their roots or their culture, but they must understand that Christianity is more than culture. Diversity is not the opposite of unity. Christianity does not deny culture; it gives it meaning and perspective. All cultures within a community or congregation should be recognized, included, and celebrated for their unique contribution to the group's identity.

Personal Layer

As we cut more deeply into the layers of racism, the outer layers can either insulate or isolate us from identifying with the problems of racism. They can help us understand how the past actions of humankind have affected us. It's easy to feel that we are not responsible for the actions of those "back there" or "out there." But racism is an individual issue as well as a national issue. As long as racism is "someone else's problem," it will remain a cancer in our churches and in our country.

Author Kyle Haselden put his finger squarely on the problem with his insightful comments:

> We are not permitted to work outward and charge the evils of prejudice to a corrupt world. We are not allowed the balms of that fatalism which blames the blind, insensitive, uncontrollable forces of history. We can only look inward and say, "my own most grievous sin." To find the guilt anywhere outside myself, to project the blame anywhere so long as I get it outside my own soul, to confer the responsibility for the removal of prejudice upon education, the law, or some other socializing agency, is merely to fortify the soul's sense of supreme innocence and superiority.[17]

By cutting through the layers of racism, our identification with this sin should cause us to weep and confess. When we cut through an onion and separate the layers with our hands, our contact with it makes us aware of our relationship to the whole. Whereas our natural tendency is to avoid the issue of racism, in doing so we contribute to its growth.

When each layer of the onion is finally removed, we discover that there is no core. Each layer, though separate from the others, is an essential part of the vegetable. Similarly, we are influenced by every layer of racism. Each is a part of what we believe and how we act. Jesus said, "What comes out of a man is what makes him unclean. For from within, out of men's hearts, come evil thoughts, sexual immorality, theft, murder, adultery, greed, malice, deceit, lewdness, envy, slander, arrogance and folly. All these evils come from inside and make a man unclean" (Mark 7:20-23). Racism is everywhere, but it comes from within.

Once we recognize the two forces that shape our thinking, attitudes, and beliefs—stereotypes and racism—and face their consequences, we can begin to assist the victims.

An article in Portland's daily newspaper featured an innovative attempt to help eliminate racism. Teenagers from around the state of Oregon were recruited for Camp Odyssey's five-day curriculum of outdoor team exercises, role-playing, workshops, and discussions aimed at exploring differences and building community. The goal for the camp was to turn the group of fifty-two students, fewer than one-half of whom were white, into people who would shun racism and sexism and share their changed values with others once they returned home. Although the teenagers experienced initial unease with one another, the program was designed to break down barriers and build trust; participants learned teamwork and problem-solving techniques during the week.

Two campers from the same hometown reportedly agreed to an antiracism and antisexism pact. If either one hears an offensive joke or comment, he has promised to speak up, and the other has pledged to support him. Those who conceived the idea of Camp Odyssey hope the seeds that were planted will take root and change the lives that those young people will touch.[18]

NOTES

1. Gordon I. Allport, *The Nature of Prejudice* (Reading, Mass.: Addison-Wesley, 1954), p. 9.

2. Arthur Lewis, "What Does the Bible Say About Mixed Marriage?" *The Standard* (June 1987): 8.

3. Pastor Emry, *What Does the Holy Bible Say?* (Phoenix, Ariz.: Lord's Covenant Church, 1969). Pamphlet.

4. Paul R. Spickard, *Mixed Blood: Intermarriage and Ethnic Identity in Twentieth-Century America* (Madison: U. of Wisconsin, 1989), p. 295.

5. Janet Groat, "Augsburg Learns Major Benefactor Sent Hostile Mail," *Minneapolis Star-Tribune*, February 16, 1988, sec. A.

6. William F. Albright, *The Old Testament World*, vol. 1 of *The Interpreter's Bible* (Nashville: Abingdon, 1952), p. 270.

7. "The Bible Speaks on Race," *The Student* (March 1984): 43.

8. Kyle Haselden, *The Racial Problem in Christian Perspective* (New York: Harper, 1959), p. 83.

9. Eugene Rivers, "Separate and Free," *Sojourners* (August/September 1990): 26.

10. Cornelius C. Tarplee, *Racial Prejudice* (Greenwich: Seabury, 1962), p. 27.

11. J. Oliver Buswell III, *Slavery, Segregation and Scripture* (Grand Rapids: Eerdmans, 1964), pp. 12-18.

12. Jim Wallis, "From Integration to Transformation," *Sojourners* (August/September 1990): 4.

13. Harold W. Cruse, "Stalled Out in History," *Sojourners* (August/September 1990): 23.

14. James E. Dittes, *Bias and the Pious* (Minneapolis: Augsburg, 1973), p. 50.

15. John Perkins, *With Justice for All* (Ventura, Calif.: Gospel Light, 1982), p. 33.

16. Alan Davies, *Infected Christianity* (Montreal: McGill-Queens U., 1988), p. 118.

17. Haselden, *Racial Problem*, pp. 85-86.

18. Andee Hochman, "Rainbow Boot Camp," *The Oregonian*, Sunday, August 19, 1990, Northwest magazine.

15. John Perkins, *With Justice for All* (Ventura, Calif.: Gospel Light, 1982), 33.
16. Alan Davies, *Infected Christianity* (Montreal: McGill Queens U., 1988), 118.
17. Haselden, *Racial Problem*, 85-86.
18. Andee Hochman, "Rainbow Boot Camp," *The Oregonian*, Sunday, 19 August 1990, Northwest magazine.

8

MIXED IDENTITY
What About the Children?

E ven though Martha and Bruce come from unrelated backgrounds and share few similarities, people asked us the same question when our children married them: "But what about their children?" Every inter-married couple has probably been asked this question. Some people assume children of mixed parentage have little chance of becoming happy, well-adjusted individuals, that they are doomed to endure confusion and hate-filled lives. The issue of intermarriage sometimes pivots around the question, "What about the children?"

Although people in general may agree that "like belongs with like," one writer states, "There is no authoritative evidence that an interracial home life is harmful to a child. . . . 'Like' is an extremely imprecise concept that covers a great deal more than skin color."[1]

When friends and acquaintances learned we had become grandparents, they often asked another question: "How dark is she?" Our answer, it seemed, determined the degree of their enthusiasm or acceptance. Family and close friends may welcome biracial children with open arms, yet society still finds them a curiosity. Soft, curly hair and warm, tan complexions confuse and intrigue people; suddenly their pigeonhole classifications no longer apply.

Society tends to think of biracial offspring as a new problem; however, statistics indicate that 75 percent of black Americans have mixed ancestry.[2] Though interracial couples may face challenges to their marriage, many have developed successful family units.

"The fact that miscegenation between two healthy people has no weakening effect on the offspring is overlooked," says Gordon Allport in *The Nature of Prejudice*. "Intermarriage cannot rationally be opposed on biological grounds. It can, however, be rationally opposed on the grounds of the handicap and conflict it could cause both parents and offspring in the present state of society. But the opposition is seldom stated in these mild terms for to do so would imply that the present state of society should be improved so that miscegenation can safely take place," Allport concludes.[3]

Many self-proclaimed tolerant and open-minded people say they are not prejudiced but remain against interracial marriage because "it is so hard on the children." That line is ridiculous, according to one author. "What white people are really saying with that statement is that they think racial prejudice is awful, especially when it affects children, and they sure are glad their kids are white!"[4]

The birth of a child frequently solidifies black/nonblack marriages when other attempts at reconciliation have failed. God often uses children in the Scriptures to illustrate the true meaning of love. He could give no clearer picture than the gift of His only Son, Jesus, to a lost world. Jesus Himself illustrated the simplicity of children: "Let the little children come to me, and do not hinder them, for the kingdom of heaven belongs to such as these" (Matthew 19:14).

Although we eventually welcomed our daughter- and son-in-law into the family, we did not become blind to our color differences until our first grandchild, Marquita, was born. When we held her tiny body in our arms, we only saw a precious child whom we welcomed with unhesitating love. Color no longer mattered; she was our flesh and blood, and we were pleased to call her ours.

According to federal statistics, about one million Americans of mixed parentage have been born here in the past twenty years. In 1987 at least 100,000 biracial children were born, as compared to 30,000 in 1968. Children of mixed parentage now represent about 3 percent of all births in the United States. In 1987 about 39 percent of mixed race children were born of black-white unions; 36 percent were Asian-white, and about 18 percent were Indian-white. The remaining 6-7 percent were mixed-race children born of Asian-black or black-Indian unions.[5]

THE IMPORTANCE OF A HEALTHY IDENTITY

We all have a need to identify to some degree with parents, family, peers, and other groups, such as religious or ethnic organizations. We wish to know how we are alike and how we differ. It is not enough just to identify with the human race; we need to feel accepted as persons.

Between the ages of three and four, most children become interested in their physical characteristics and compare themselves with others. They notice hair color, skin tone, and people who wear glasses or are physically handicapped. Their questions need to be answered honestly and accurately by parents and teachers; they shouldn't be avoided or passed off as trivial. It is important to point out to children that physical characteristics are inherited from both parents. This may be done naturally while looking through family photo albums or magazines. Simply point out similarities and differences, making sure to communicate that physical differences are neither good nor bad.

"Did you know there are two Negroes in my class?" our son Scott informed us the day he brought home a picture of his kindergarten class.

"Which ones are they?" asked Anita, unaware of any black children in his class.

"There's one . . . and there's one," Scott answered, pointing to two children.

Anita explained to Scott that both children were Mexican-American. She then asked him if he thought anyone else in the picture was a Negro.

"Nope," Scott answered, after taking a closer look. "That's all."

"What about her?" Anita questioned as she pointed to his African-American teacher.

"No-o-o, Mom!" he replied. "That's my teacher."

Scott had not only misidentified the two Hispanic students, but he hadn't realized his teacher was black. His relationship with his teacher was more important than the pigmentation of her skin.

Although society will always try to label people, no one should have to reject any of his or her heritage to fit into society's categories. Some biracial children may choose to call themselves "black," whereas others may want to be identified as "mixed," "biracial," "brown," or "tan." Their right to choose what they wish to be called must be granted, whether it be on an application form, a census survey, or in conversation.

Jewelle Gibbs, a clinical psychologist and associate professor at the University of California at Berkeley, says the mixed-race child will want to identify with a white parent instead of a minority parent, at least until adolescence. "But particularly at adolescence reality sinks in that society labels and defines you as a minority," says Gibbs. "That's when a lot of problems begin for a mixed-race child—feeling ambivalent about identity, like a marginal person, having torn loyalties." The child's sense of identity shifts from the majority group to the minority group about that time.[6]

On the other hand, the identity of young children may more often come from the parent (black or white) with whom the child spends the most time.

Many light-skinned blacks carry the burden of their heritage on the outside for all humanity to see. Some feel like misfits and try to be something they are not. They need to be respected, not because of their ancestry or the color of their skin, but because they are individuals with distinct personalities.

Langston Hughes illustrates his confusion as a biracial child through poetry:

Cross

My old man's a white old man
And my old mother's black.
If ever I cursed my white old man
I take my curses back.

If ever I cursed my black old mother
And wished she were in hell,
I'm sorry for the evil wish
And now I wish her well.

My old man died in a fine big house,
My ma died in a shack,
I wonder where I'm gonna die,
Being neither white nor black.[7]

From *Selected Poems of Langston Hughes* by Langston Hughes. Copyright 1926 by Alfred A. Knopf, Inc. and renewed 1954 by Langston Hughes. Reprinted by permission of the publisher.

The situation does not have to be discouraging. Paul L. Adams, a physician and counselor, believes that though biracial children face more difficult adjustments growing up than do children from homogeneous homes, their perspective is "broader than the mass of either white or black children." According to Adams, they are

> keenly imaginative and perceptive . . . in their world view, more astute socially, and more clever than either the average black or the average white child. . . . To know from one's birth and to grow up with parents who have broken some conventions and who have not observed the taboos, may conceivably give one some advantages for living in the world today.[8]

What Parents Can Do

Often society forces biracial children to function between two worlds with two sets of expectations. Although they may learn to behave appropriately in the black as well as the white community, they constantly juggle their mode of behavior and struggle to be themselves. In *Interracial Marriage: Expectations and Realities* this struggle is aptly described:

> The burden of a black-white child is infinitely greater [than that of a black child]. [Mixed children] are poised between two worlds, two sets of expectations, and they are sometimes ravaged by conflict. Such a child is in conflict with parents, with society, and with himself. *How well biracial children are able to resolve their struggle, depends upon the awareness of parents and their ability to integrate this conflict for the child.* [Italics added][9]

Parents of mixed youngsters have a complicated task. They must be comfortable with their own racial identity in order to teach their offspring to respect their mixed heritage. Biracial children should be able to feel good about their cultural background, not embarrassed or apologetic. It is up to parents to help their children form a positive identity if they are to become healthy, proud families.

Psychologist James Jacobs, a white father of two interracial children, says, "A lot of parents, because of their own insecurities or their own painful experiences involving race, can be rather avoidant and hesitant about seeing their child upset as the child begins in his own self to understand who he is. In some cases, parents may be hurt if a child identifies with their race, but expresses ambivalence or negative feelings about it, such as wishing one's hair were straight or more curly."[10] Children should be free to choose their own identity without worrying about taking sides or offending either parent.

Family sociologist Joyce Ladner says, "Love is not enough. [Biracial children] must be prepared to cope. How well these kids succeed depends largely on their parents, who must warn the youngsters about the discriminatory restrictions that may be in store for them, while at the same time teaching them about all aspects of their racial character."[11]

She states that parents tend to deal with racial identity from three basic perspectives: *human, biracial,* or *black.* Some parents believe that color is totally irrelevant, that people should be seen as human beings, not assigned to distinct groups. According to Ladner, this attitude isn't realistic because society in fact treats their child as if he is black.

Other parents stress their children's biracial identity. But the question here, according to Ladner, is "how to teach black pride without diminishing the other part of a child's heritage." Traditions and customs from both parents should be incorporated into the family.

A third group of parents teach their children to adopt a black identity and immerse themselves totally in black communities, denying or ignoring the other side of their heritage. Blacks may expect the children to act black, and they may be criticized for not performing according to those expectations.

But how does a black child act? Many behavior patterns are generated by culture, not color. Although genetic characteristics sometimes exist (i.e., bone structure and coordination may create a gifted athlete), behavior cannot be predicted on the basis of skin color. Biracial children know they are not perceived as white, so they are caught in a dilemma. As a result, interracial families may be more comfortable living in multiethnic communities, where their children can develop a positive identity. People in such neighborhoods are accustomed to seeing different cultures and colors of skin, and they don't look at interracial families as abnormal.

Children born of black-Asian, black-American Indian, and black-Hispanic unions must learn the same coping skills, for they, too, carry a stigma and will be seen by society as "black."

How the Family Can Help

Experts tell us that an infant can sense acceptance or rejection by "reading" the muscular tone, vocal tension, breathing, and heart rate of his mother. Interracial families also sense rejection and disapproval when they "read" expressions of curiosity or disgust from staring eyes in shopping malls and restaurants or disapproving glances of passersby. Some families choose to ignore these offenses whereas other families isolate themselves to avoid conflict or abuse. It is important for interracial families to come to grips with the social factor and learn to cope with the complexities their children may face.

Although some people view interracial families with interest, curiosity, or even outright hostility, "we must support our children's unique status in society," says Francis Wardle. He cautions families not to shrink into the woodwork but to voice strong disagreement to notions that their children are marginal, mixed-up, or unable to fit in. Wardle stresses that parents must "demand that [their children] are normal, and that professionals and institutions adjust their antiquated notions to meet the real needs of [their] children."[12]

All concerned parents teach their children to be confident and strong, develop good relationships, and respect others, but minority parents must also teach their children how to handle racial conflicts. "The struggle to bring up black children who understand the unfairness of racism but will not be paralyzed or embittered by it is at the heart of the civil rights movement today," declares Juan Williams of the *Washington Post*. "And the crux of that struggle is the goal of bringing up black children who will be strong enough as adults to form stable, happy black families."[13]

Anita learned to fear dark-skinned people from her father's comments and warnings. Although he may have been concerned primarily for his family's safety, her father instilled a lasting fear in his children. Fear of strangers is a natural fear, so parents should purposely expose children to various people groups to teach them about the world in which they live. This can be done by entertaining international students, studying mission fields, joining inner-city clubs for children, such as the YMCA, Scouts, or museum programs. When children learn to know and trust people from different backgrounds, it's easier for parents to discuss the inappropriateness of name-calling and racism.

We misunderstand and fear each other because we do not know one another. People of different races may work together, attend the same schools and churches, and even live in the same neighborhoods, but until they begin to associate with each other as friends and equals, it is difficult to develop brotherly love.

If racism really begins in the home as many experts claim, the home is where we must endeavor to effect change. Exposing children to people who are different from them is only a beginning. Beyond that, parents can encourage relationships between their children and children of other races and see that they play together. Parents need to display nonverbal acceptance and set good examples for their kids. Eye contact, a friendly smile, a warm greeting, and a hearty handshake exhibit genuine acceptance.

According to the authors of *Intermarriage in the United States,*

> a child born of an intermarriage may find it difficult to integrate into either parents' social group. However, what an individual loses in comfort and integration he may gain in insight and understanding of both groups. As more children of interracial couples take on a biracial identity, there may increasingly be enough others in his similar situation that he may lose his sense of uniqueness and isolation.[14]

Until then, teachers, social workers, and other professionals may view biracial children's problems as a result of the interracial nature of their families, even though the problems may be due, instead, to other difficulties. Parents must prepare their children for the cruel realities of racism and at the same time assure them of their love and support.

Alvin Poussaint told a conference on interracial children, "We have lots of reasons to suspect that an interracial background can be an advantage to children in this society. Not only are they high achievers, but also socially they are adept at forming friendships with both black and white peers."[15]

Many of today's youth—including our own children —are more tolerant and accepting of interracial marriage than have been previous generations. Although polls show that younger whites are more likely to live, work, and socialize in racially mixed atmospheres and have close friends who are black than are older generations, that does not suggest that more young people will necessarily choose to marry across racial lines. We do not propose interracial marriage as a cure-all to the problem of racism, but young people can teach us a great deal. In our family they have taught us to unlearn some of the trappings and biases of our upbringing and re-evaluate the attributes we formerly admired.

It is our prayer that we learn to see people as individuals—not as blacks, whites, Asians, or Hispanics but as God's creation and worthy of respect. We had to uncover layers of prejudice from our lives before we could begin to see that every person—adult or child—is of eternal value to our heavenly Father, the Creator of us all. We also must allow Him to work in other people's hearts as He has worked in ours. Our education, although sometimes painful, has brought greater understanding and richer rewards than we ever dreamed possible. Until people learn to appreciate and respect one another rather than belittle and judge each other for things that cannot be changed, we must agree with Kate Shackford, a mother of two interracial children who said, "Ultimately . . . the problems interracial children face will be solved only when racism is eradicated."[16]

The need for love and self-worth cannot be minimized; it is inherent in every human being. Children must feel wanted and important to their parents in order to develop a positive self-concept. How can responsible parents do any less than love our children and

grandchildren completely and see them as God does—
worthwhile and full of promise?

NOTES

1. "Are Interracial Homes Bad for Children?" in *Marriage Across the Color Line*, ed. Cloyte M. Larsson (Chicago: Johnson, 1965), p. 68.
2. Alvin F. Poussaint, "Study of Interracial Children Presents Positive Picture," *Interracial Books for Children Bulletin* 15, no. 6 (1984): 9-10.
3. Gordon I. Allport, *The Nature of Prejudice* (Reading, Mass.: Addison-Wesley, 1954), p. 376.
4. Lee Channult, "Negro Child, White Mother," in *Marriage Across the Color Line*, ed. Cloyte M. Larsson (Chicago: Johnson, 1965), p. 87.
5. Felicity Barringer, "Mixed-Race Generation Emerges But Is Not Sure Where It Fits," *New York Times*, September 24, 1989.
6. Ibid.
7. Langston Hughes, "Cross," in *Selected Poems of Langston Hughes* (New York: Alfred A. Knopf, 1926). Used by permission.
8. Paul L. Adams, M.D., "Counseling with Interracial Couples and Their Children in the South," in *Interracial Marriage: Expectations and Realities*, eds. Irvin R. Stuart and Lawrence E. Abt (New York: Grossman, 1973), p. 76.
9. Irvin R. Stuart and Lawrence E. Abt, eds., *Interracial Marriage: Expectations and Realities* (New York: Grossman, 1973), p. 321.
10. Joyce Ladner, "Children of the Rainbow," *Newsweek* (November 19, 1984): 120.
11. Ibid.
12. Francis Wardle, "Raising Good Biracial Children," *Interrace* (January 1990): 23.
13. Juan Williams, "The Color of Their Skin," *Parenting* (March 1988): 49-53.
14. Gary A. Cretser and Joseph Leon, eds., *Intermarriage in the United States: Marriage and Family Review* 5, no. 1 (New York: Haworth, 1982), p. 111.
15. Lynn Norment, "Children of Interracial Marriages," *Ebony* (September 1985): 156-162.
16. Kate Shackford, "Interracial Children: Growing Up Healthy in an Unhealthy Society," *Interracial Books for Children Bulletin* 15, no. 6 (1984): 6.

9

MIXED SUPPORT

After They Say, "I Do"

D o you think their marriage will last?" Anita was asked several weeks after Mark and Martha's wedding.

Her mother bear instincts readied for attack. "It had better last!" she snapped. "And we'll do everything we can to make sure it does. After all, they've made a commitment!"

Regardless of our initial hesitancy, once our children married we stood by them 100 percent. Mark and Martha's promise to God took precedence over any personal feelings we had. The same commitment to the sanctity of marriage that sealed our own wedding vows would sustain Mark and Martha through the years ahead.

Martha and Bruce were believers in Jesus Christ; that was what mattered most. By the time our children recited their marriage vows, race no longer took center stage. Through God's patient teaching we learned to respect their choices of marriage partners and to accept Martha and Bruce as part of God's perfect plan.

Interracial couples don't always have the blessing of family and friends; some feel alienated and separated at a time when confirmation of their love and support of their decision to marry is most important. Some couples never completely reconcile with their families, whereas others find that gradual healing takes place as everyone gets better acquainted.

Although it is often assumed that interracial marriages suffer far higher divorce rates, author-historian Paul Spickard reports the results of studies on this issue: "There is no evidence to indicate that the divorce rate is higher among the intermarried than in the population as a whole; indeed there is reason to think that the reverse may be true. The fact that they have violated a taboo together may well act as an additional bond between interracial couples."[1]

Building relationships between in-laws (black or white) requires much time and prayer. The resulting benefits, however, always make the effort worthwhile. Since we come from a very different world than both Martha and Bruce, we've had much to unlearn. We've never experienced outright hatred due to the color of our skin, nor have we been forced to stay home because rioters threatened to charge through the doors of our school. We have not walked in their shoes.

Martha admits to being a shy and terrified young woman when we first met. Not only were we in-laws, we were white in-laws. We began immediately to include her in every letter we wrote, even placing her name first, as in "Dear Martha and Mark." Perhaps we were a bit oversensitive, but we didn't want to give Martha any reason to believe that she held a lesser place in our hearts. Trust and love increasingly developed, especially after our son and his wife were transferred back to the United States.

We are often reminded of our difficulty in finding appropriate engagement and wedding cards for our children. So far, Hallmark hasn't designed greeting cards for interracial families. Refusing to purchase cards that portrayed either white or black couples, we eventually settled on those which depicted lovers walking off in the distance, hand in hand. Our selection of greeting cards continues to be limited to pictures of flowers, landscapes, or cute little animals, unless we purposely seek out shops in mixed neighborhoods or remember to order cards in advance from specialty catalogs.

Early in their marriage, God used an innocent remark of Martha's to endear her to us. She simply said, "When I have a child . . . " Her words and facial expression were loving and tender as she spoke the words. She hadn't said, "when I get pregnant," but, "when I have a child." The thought of her child one day being our flesh and blood hastened the bonding process for us.

Similarly, we found it hard to resist Bruce's impeccable manners when we received a lovely floral arrangement from him for our Thanksgiving dinner table. His prompt and cordial thank-you notes would have made any parent proud. It's difficult to admit, but our children and their spouses have taught us that although we weren't racists, we were prejudiced and needed to change some of our thinking.

Charles Moody, founder of the National Alliance of Black School Educators, challenges each of us to take a step toward erasing racism:

> People must accept the fact that racism exists and begin to do something about it. I think people as individuals can do something about it by looking at themselves and trying to change that part of the institution or community that they have control over. All of us have control over some part of it, even if it is just ourselves. . . . People have to stop thinking, "How can I promote equality without losing my advantage?" and acknowledge that one group of people can't just continue to enjoy advantages as if they are a God-given right.[2]

"But what can I do?" you may ask. Perhaps some of the suggestions in this chapter will encourage you to speak out, take action, or befriend a neighbor. If more Christians would dare to interrupt a racial or ethnic joke or take issue with a bigoted remark, people might begin to think twice before they repeat careless comments and stories.

Our younger son, Scott, is the least prejudiced person we know. He simply enjoys people. He's a school bus driver and is pursuing a degree in American Indian studies at the University of Minnesota. His bus route travels through poverty pockets of Minneapolis where he picks up children of a variety of racial and ethnic backgrounds. One day as the children boarded his bus, an American Indian boy called another child a "chink."

"Why did you call him that?" questioned Scott.

"He talks funny," the boy answered.

"How many languages can you speak?"

"One. So what?"

"Well, that boy can speak two languages. So don't go calling him names, OK?" Scott replied.

Granted, that brief conversation didn't allow Scott to elaborate on the evils of racism or stereotyping. But when he pointed out the wrongness of name-calling, he did something to change the small part of his world over which he had some control.

A sense of humor also helps. Debby and Bruce almost changed their china pattern when they discovered it was called "Ivory and Ebony." "People will think we purposely chose it because of the name," Debby said when she read the pattern title on the back of a plate. But she and Bruce decided to keep the pattern and laugh at comments as they came.

Other people help by establishing organizations and publishing newsletters for interracial families. Mary Murchison-Edwords organized the Interracial Club of Buffalo, New York in 1983. "The subject of interracial marriages is one no one talks about. It's like we don't even exist," says Murchison-Edwords. "We just want to feel comfortable. It's nice to be in numbers."[3]

Subjects of interest range from creating an environment in which the family bond is fostered, to recognizing and affirming the interracial/intercultural family as a viable family unit, to forums for education, which may cover single parenting, caring for a child's tight, curly hair, and developing self-esteem in a child.

Interracial organizations offer encouragement to many families. They provide opportunity for adults and children to mix socially with people like themselves where they are perceived not as oddities but as ordinary human beings. (See the list of interracial organizations at the back of the book.)

We surveyed more than one hundred interracial and intercultural couples about their greatest concerns. The most important concern was meeting the needs of their children. Though the responsibilities of biracial parenting may seem staggering, parents need not despair. Successful parenting of biracial children follows the same guidelines as all good parenting. Every child needs confidence, acceptance, and love. "Despite the problem . . . biracial children can—and do—grow up in a healthy environment," says Joyce Ladner.[4]

"Children in biracial families need everything that all other children need. However, in some ways their needs are unique," explains Paula Phillips, director of the Bi-Racial Families Resource Center. Phillips suggests that biracial children need open discussions of racial issues, guidance for handling difficult situations, and accurate information given in age-appropriate ways about racism and how it might affect them. She strongly urges exposing children to individuals and groups who are working to create a society with "racial justice and freedom for all people to be who they are."[5]

Children should be able to talk openly with parents and teachers about difficult experiences. They need assurance that they are good and beautiful. Parents should meet with teachers to discuss how they wish their child's heritage to be treated. Families are encouraged to celebrate various cultural and racial heritages in the home as well as in the community. Role models are important for children to develop self-esteem and pride. Parents and teachers should point to examples of minority or mixed-race individuals who have made a contribution to society, such as public servants, athletes, musicians, and authors.

We subscribe to several newsletters from interracial organizations and find their articles to be valuable resources. Through these newsletters we learn about court actions, new articles and books, television programs, and films. We've also discovered ethnic games, toys, and books for children, as well as catalogs and other related materials. Although much of the newsletter material is of local interest, many articles also relate to the multicultural society in which we live.

"We must prepare our children to live and work harmoniously and productively in an increasingly multicultural and multiracial society," states the National Parent Teachers Association.[6]

When some friends moved from a large city to a rural community, the other children in the new school wouldn't play with their five-year-old daughter, claiming she was "black." The little girl, a child of a white father and white/Korean mother, was the only minority in the school. The situation presented a perfect opportunity for parents and teachers to address the subject of prejudice and unfairness, even at the kindergarten level. We must find out what creates children's misconceptions in order to correct them.

Children who never see Hispanics and blacks in normal family living situations, observing them only in negative roles on television and in the news media, may assume that all minorities are "bad." Some children may overhear those same groups slandered in demeaning jokes and comments and then draw negative, stereotypical conclusions. Public pressure has brought some change to television programming in recent years (such as casting minority actors in advertisements and "good guy" roles), but we still have a long way to go.

Concerned Christians have an obligation to respond to children. If we never address the unfairness of racial slurs and jokes, children may grow up believing that anyone who is different from them is inferior and doesn't deserve to be treated equally.

The National PTA suggests possible responses to children's racial comments. Respond with a simple, "I see why you said that, but that's not really the way I see it." Be direct. Be brief. Use language the child will understand. The following are suggested discussions:

> Question: Why do some people call others bad names?
> Answer: Name-calling hurts, doesn't it? Some people grow up with foolish ideas that they are better than other people just because of their skin color or where they live. But when children like you grow up, differences will become less and less important.
> Question: Why do those people act funny?
> Answer: Aren't you glad everyone isn't just alike? I bet we seem funny to them. We live in an interesting world where we can learn things from many different people.[7]

"One of the most important things a parent [or teacher] can do is communicate a respect for differ-

ences," stresses Gerald Lesser, Harvard University professor of education and one of the creators of Sesame
Street. He makes several suggestions to parents.

Be honest. "Admit you may have some racist ten-
dencies."

Don't be naive. "Your child will pick up on those little comments you make."

Be wary of mixed messages. "If you invite a black
child to your kid's birthday party, make sure he isn't
simply there as a token."

Don't avoid dialogue. "Parents have the responsibility to address the issue of racism and to pass on a sense
of good and bad in all races."[8]

Parents must also teach their children how to stand
up for themselves, protect themselves, and maintain
pride in who they are.

One little girl was overheard saying to her playmate, "I'm brown." She then stretched out her arm and
said, "See. Look for yourself." Another youngster casu-
ally calls himself "beige" when explaining his biracial
heritage. The point is, children can be ready to respond
with pride when necessary.

"People with European backgrounds have always
talked about their combined heritages—sometimes
with humor, often with pride," says Francis Wardle.
"Parents of mixed ethnic children are now doing the
same. It's not a question of race. It's a question of both
parents believing their cultures and heritages are important to their child's growth and identity." Wardle
also suggests that parents expose children to both sets
of grandparents and other relatives.[9]

Parents should meet with teachers as early as the
day-care level to discuss how they would prefer to have
their child's heritage dealt with at school. Sunday school
teachers and club leaders can also help to ensure con-

stant reinforcement of a child's positive identity. Wise teachers will find ways to change that segment of the community over which they have some control and weave the rich cultures represented by their students into lesson materials.

The Council on Interracial Books for Children offers the following guidelines for choosing reading material for children:

1. Check illustrations. Are minorities portrayed in subservient roles? Are blacks drawn as whites, then tinted with brown ink?
2. Scrutinize the story line. Is being successful in white society projected as the only ideal? Are minorities considered part of the story's problem?
3. Look at lifestyles. Are minorities seen living only in ghettos and barrios? Is clothing stereotyped?
4. Weigh interpersonal relationships. Do whites make all the important decisions? Are Hispanic mothers over-laden with children? Do black mothers rule the home?
5. Watch heroes. Are minority heroes admired for the same qualities as white heroes or because what they did benefited white people?
6. Consider the child's self-image. Do boys and men perform the brave and important deeds? Are there minority characters with positive attributes for minority children to identify with?
7. Check the author's background. Is there anything that qualifies the author to write sensitively and accurately about a particular race? Does the author's socioeconomic background—traditionally white and middle class—affect the work's value?
8. Watch for loaded words.
9. Look at the copyright date. In the 1960s a flood of "minority experience" books were written and edited by whites. For the most part, they do nothing to enlighten or smash stereotypes.[10]

America has been described as a melting pot where immigrants gradually drop their former languages and cultures to take on the vocabulary and customs of the majority. Rather than one giant melting pot, a more accurate description of today's America is a "stew pot."[11]

C. Peter Wagner elaborates on that metaphor in his book *Our Kind of People.* "In a stew pot, each ingredient adds its characteristic flavor to every other ingredient, but all maintain their own identities and integrity. The final result is more than the sum of the parts. It is a new product, colorful and flavorful to a degree that would have been impossible for any of the ingredients taken alone."[12]

Young people need to develop skills to feel at home in today's multiracial, multicultural society. "The black-white child's struggle with himself, his parents, society and with his past and present elicits our respect, admiration, and compassion," write authors Irving Stuart and Lawrence Abt. "These families' successes are our hopes—their failures our warnings."[13]

Community organizations can cooperate in helping to meet immediate needs by providing funding and forums whereby better understanding between people groups is made possible. Interracial couples themselves can help others develop positive racial attitudes by sinking their roots into the community through neighborhood schools and churches. Positive models, such as grandparents, business owners, doctors, and school principals, demonstrate to young people that they don't have to be the "bad guys."

Many changes have occurred in our own lives as we've gotten to know people of other races and cultures. We entered the picture cautiously, "walking on tiptoes," unsure of who we might offend or how we might be received. Though much of what we've learned over the past nine years has been through trial and error, common sense and a healthy respect for all individuals has usually put us in good stead. Support for intermarried couples and their children will undoubtedly continue to be mixed. How you respond to these families will make a difference in their lives as well as in your own.

NOTES

1. Paul R. Spickard, *Mixed Blood: Intermarriage and Ethnic Identity in Twentieth-Century America* (Madison: U. of Wisconsin, 1989), p. 359.

2. Charles Moody, Sr., "Individuals Can Do Something," *U.S.A. Today* (September 11, 1989): 6A.

3. Judy Kay, "It's Spelled Out in Black and White," *Niagara Gazette*, February 7, 1983.

4. Joyce Ladner, "Providing a Healthy Environment for Interracial Children," *Interracial Books for Children Bulletin* 15, no. 6 (1984): 8.

5. Paula Phillips, "What Do Interracial Children Need?" *Interracial Books for Children Bulletin* 15, no. 6 (1984): 8.

6. *What to Tell Your Child About Prejudice and Discrimination*, the National PTA and the Anti-Defamation League of B'nai B'rith, 1989.

7. Ibid.

8. Marco R. della Cava, "Parents Have the Power to Raise Colorblind Children," *U.S.A. Today* (September 18, 1989): 5D.

9. Francis Wardle, "What Is the Identity of Children with a Mixed Heritage?" in *Parenting* newsletter 10, no. 5 (May 1987): 1.

10. Marco R. della Cava, "Choosing Sensitive Reading Material," *U.S.A. Today* (September 18, 1989): 5D.

11. Andrew M. Greeley, "Catholics Prosper While the Church Crumbles," *Psychology Today* (June 1976): 44.

12. C. Peter Wagner, *Our Kind of People* (Atlanta: John Knox, 1979), p. 51.

13. Irvin R. Stuart and Lawrence E. Abt, eds., *Interracial Marriage: Expectations and Realities* (New York: Grossman, 1973), p. 61.

10

MIXED IMAGES
Getting the Whole Picture

Fred attended a multicultural workshop in 1989, where participants represented many theological persuasions and denominations. Having been in similar settings before, he was prepared for the extreme range of beliefs and opinions that would be expressed. But one event was so unusual that it overshadowed all other discussion.

One evening, rather than discussing racism in a classroom, the participants traveled to various churches on the south side of Chicago to listen to leaders explain how they handled racism. Fred's group was scheduled to spend an evening with an African-American church whose motto was "Unashamedly black and unapologetically Christian." The Wednesday night activities had already begun when the group arrived at the church. A policeman directed traffic out in front as crowds of people made their way into the building.

The group was ushered into a large room and welcomed by the church leaders. They listened for the next two hours as one person after another explained his or her African Christian heritage. Although the church welcomed whites to their services, there was no question that the focus and activities emphasized a black religious experience for the parishioners. That evening Fred realized that his previous exposure to black Christians and their views had been totally inadequate. The experience challenged his ethnocentrism and theological views.

As Fred's group returned to the conference center, all discussion focused on a painting that hung in the church foyer. The picture portrayed Jesus standing behind a family with His hands resting on the parents' shoulders. The family consisted of a mother and father, son and daughter. All five people in the painting, including Jesus, were black. Whereas the picture had a profound affect on the white theologians, Fred's immediate response was reactionary. "Jesus wasn't black. He was white!"

Or was He? The more those theologians discussed the color of Jesus' skin, the more obvious it became that previously they had only seen Jesus portrayed as white-skinned.

Perhaps that painting portraying Jesus' skin color as swarthy was more accurate than most white Christians' assumptions. But does it really matter what color of paint the artist uses? Is our traditional image of a white Jesus truly important to our theology or racial views?

The fact that Jesus was black was not what initiated most of the theologians' discussion, however. The other participants were actually more disturbed by the fact that the parents and children all had black skin. In order to correctly represent God's family, they argued, one child should have had white skin and the other black. Yet logically how could the children have different skin colors if both parents were black?

Until that evening, the only similar pictures Fred had seen were ones of Jesus with an entirely white family or of Jesus with a number of children of different coloring standing around Him, and no parents. Would any church dare to hang a picture of Jesus, regardless of His skin color, standing with an interracial family, the parents being black and white and the children of varying skin tones?

Whereas the majority of American churches picture Jesus with a European-American family, some picture Him with a black family. Others may paint a Native American Jesus and family, an Asian-American Jesus and family, or a Hispanic Jesus and family. Perhaps pictures should be large enough to include Jesus with a variety of families representing all the colors of the rainbow.

Generally church congregations will be most comfortable with a picture of Jesus standing beside a family with the same skin color as the congregation. The question still persists, however: Does it really matter what color the skin is? Is our mental picture of the Christian family broad enough to include parents of different races and biracial children?

The basic question here is not what kind of picture hangs in our church foyer or sanctuary. Instead we need to ask, "Are we willing to accept all families in our pews? Will they be accepted into our fellowship circles or only on our membership rolls?"

What does the family of God look like? We have a description from John of what to expect: "After this I looked and there before me was a great multitude that no one could count, from every nation, tribe, people and language, standing before the throne and in front of the Lamb" (Revelation 7:9). An accurate picture of the heavenly family is one that is multiracial, multiethnic, and multicultural.

Since that eternal picture includes diversity, the church should resemble that illustration. Jesus taught His disciples to pray, "Your kingdom come, your will be done on earth as it is in heaven" (Matthew 6:9).

Considering the Christian beliefs of brotherhood and equality, it is baffling that churches haven't been in the vanguard of integrative philosophy. Before castigating the church for its unwillingness or inability to integrate, however, it is essential to note that many individual churches have succeeded in bringing racial and ethnic groups together. We've attended and read about churches that have intentionally developed a strategy based on unity through diversity.

Why has the elimination of racism been relegated to such a low place (if any at all) on the church's agenda? Unfortunately the vast number of churches view racism as a problem that does not involve them. Basically we have covered ourselves with a blanket of silence. Racial issues are not even discussed, let alone debated or decided upon, at church business meetings. Attitudes and beliefs form the foundation for activity (or inactivity); activity does not determine beliefs. Although individual church members and families do speak out against racism, overall churches tend to present a weak and uncertain message.

Why do we remain silent on this important issue? Perhaps one reason is the assumption that racism is no longer a problem in America as explained in an article in *His* magazine:

> The demise of public segregation, the increase of middle-class blacks, the heightened sense of Black Consciousness, and the fading of the Civil Rights Movement have combined to give the illusion that we have made substantial progress in overcoming racism.[1]

But laws and external solutions cannot eliminate problems in the church. Racism should not be left to society to solve. It is a spiritual problem that Christians need to address.

Another reason churches remain silent has to do with the location of individual churches. Many communities are isolated from people who are racially or culturally different. So racism is somewhere else—South Africa, the rural South, or urban North. Because racism seems so distant, congregations tend to wrestle with other more "immediate" sins—atheism, humanism, materialism, and so on.

Perhaps the biggest reason for silence is our failure to preach the whole gospel. Sermons are not preached, Sunday school lessons are not taught, and questions are not raised on the subject of racism. Some churches have delegated all controversial social issues to committees, such as a "Social Concerns Committee." Although the people who are genuinely concerned get involved, the issue is relegated to study and concern instead of action.[2]

Someone wrote "Jesus is the answer" on a classroom blackboard. The next day a second line was written below: "But what are the questions?" Christians believe that Jesus is the answer to all of humankind's problems, so silence and indifference can never be a suitable answer to the sins of our generation.

Churches that consciously or unconsciously avoid discussion on racial issues, refrain from responding to injustice, and avoid neighborhoods where racial and cultural diversity exist are guilty of preaching a partial gospel. If we are to reach the whole world with the whole gospel, we cannot be selective lovers.

Some churches say they are integrated, but only one or two individuals or families of a minority race attend. Fred once asked a black pastor from Portland, "How many integrated churches are there in the Portland area?"

"There are many biracial churches," he replied, "but only a few integrated ones."

A biracial congregation is where people of different races and cultures worship together at the same church. After the benediction is pronounced, however, there is seldom any social interaction. People who sit next to each other in church on Sunday morning may have no further social contact during the week. In that respect churches are no different from the rest of American society. A special report by *Newsweek* describes racial relationships: "Blacks and whites now more often work together, lunch together, even live side by side, yet few really count each other as friends. 'It is an integrated America only to the extent that we have to come in contact with one another,' says Donald Hill, a black professor at Texas Southern University. 'After five o'clock at night, whites and blacks retreat to their own isolated worlds.'"[3]

Integration within churches is not only a white problem. Whereas whites still talk about the advances of integration in the 1990s, many people of color question the benefits of those advances. A special report on the "Separation of Church" by the *Seattle Times* describes this shift: "In a kind of a role reversal, it is sometimes whites who talk about integration, while people of color benefit in their Sunday refuge from a white world."[4] This retreat from integration has been adopted by many congregations composed of new immigrants as well.

The new separation is seen by its detractors as a euphemism for the old segregation. They perceive it as a step backward in attempts to achieve racial harmony. Ethnic and racial groups throughout American history used to worship separately because of language barriers. Most of those congregations in the late nineteenth century and through the first half of the twentieth century aimed to be assimilated into mainstream American culture. In contrast, many churches today desire to maintain both their native language and their national cultures.

Separation differs, however, from our former emphasis on segregation. Separation is based on the desire of racial and ethnic groups to preserve their culture and heritage. Although they are intentionally focused in their cultural emphasis, they do not attempt to exclude others who want to be part of their particular cultural expression. But the fact remains, segregation and separation, though different in focus, both result in keeping Christians isolated from each other.

Another concept that has had an adverse effect on integration of the church has been homogeneity. Church growth experts believe that churches grow faster numerically when they adopt the "homogeneous unit" principle. History and current experience document the fact that churches usually grow more quickly when they are composed of the same kinds of people. Church attenders are attracted to places where congregations have similar roots, practice the same customs, and worship the same way they do.

Those whose goal is pluralism in the local church point to the New Testament pattern of congregations of diverse people, where people of racial and socioeconomic differences worshiped together. Promoters of separation in local congregations are not biblical in their approach, they say. Regardless of whether the separatist approach derives its philosophy from a goal of cultural heritage or a goal of church growth, separation should not flourish in the church.

Racial diversity and cultural differences do not need to destroy racial harmony. As the church approaches the twenty-first century, it should refrain from constructing additional barriers. Unless we begin to tear down walls, the church itself will lose its potential impact on the world.

Joel Gregory, pastor of the First Baptist Church in Dallas, tells a story of a businessman from the United States who wanted to buy a castle. During a trip to the British Isles, he found a castle that was for sale. He purchased the property, even though some stones were missing from the building and repairs were needed. In order to prevent additional damage to his castle, the businessman hired a stonemason to build a wall to protect his investment. Before going back to the United States, he told the stonemason to notify him when the wall was completed so that he could return to Scotland to inspect it.

The businessman was pleased to know that pilfering from his castle would soon be eliminated. Upon completion of the wall, he eagerly returned to his property. The new wall met with his approval, but when he walked through the gate to view his castle, the businessman could not believe his eyes. The building was gone! The stonemason had taken the stones from the castle to build the wall.

Sometimes we destroy the very institutions we are trying to protect by building walls around them. Christ came to break down the wall of sin that separates us from God; He also came to destroy the walls that separate His people from each other. In Ephesians 2:14 Paul states that Christ "destroyed the barrier, the dividing wall of hostility" between Jews and Gentile. Building walls cannot be justified when those walls destroy the church.

In a survey of its readers *Christianity Today* asked, "If you favor more integration in the church, who do you think has the major responsibility to work toward this?" Eighty-eight percent of the respondents indicated it was the responsibility of the local church to take the initiative.[5]

Evangelical churches possess the power and resources to combat racism. "The blame and the remedy for our social evils [belong] on the shoulders of the 40 million evangelicals in this country. If we can't solve the problem of racism in our churches, what right do we have to pontificate to the world?"[6]

How can Christians work together when churches choose separation? Racial healing demands that churches work together. Perhaps rather than pursue a policy of integration within the local church, Christians should attempt a policy of synergism among churches. Synergism is "interaction so that the total effect is greater than the sum of the individual effects." Intrachurch relationships, as well as interchurch relationships, should seek the same goals.

It is our prayer and hope that churches of all denominations and cultural, ethnic, and racial backgrounds will begin to follow the example and commands of Jesus Christ concerning the oneness of His people. A synergistic approach simply means that Christians, whatever their orientation, begin the process toward racial harmony. There is no "quick fix" to the problem of racism.

Synergism is both a process and a product. Sometimes it is easy to forget that the process is as important as the product. Michael Verchot, a member of Sojourners Community Church, gives refreshing advice to churches who want to take steps toward racial justice:

> Because the sin of racism is so deep and pervasive, we can not expect to overcome it quickly. . . . Try to involve the entire church (not just the social concerns committee), and try to make the events flow out of the life of the congregation. Second, this step must lead to another one. A single event will not complete the task.[7]

Steps Toward Racial Unity

Several steps form a synergistic process that can guide churches toward racial unity. But whose responsibility is it to take the initiative? Prejudice does not belong exclusively to the white church. Any church, no matter what its race or ethnic background, can be guilty of racial discrimination and bigotry. However, white churches, because of their past sins of slavery and segregation and their continuing acts of injustice, both conscious and unconscious, need to accept the responsibility to begin the healing process. We see five basic steps in this process.

REPENTING

Since racism is a sin, repentance is the first step in dealing with this deep and widespread offense. To begin, white people should repent of the sins of the past. Although we weren't alive when racial sins against Native and black Americans were committed, and we can't go back into history to right those wrongs, racism against these two groups continues today. Just as all Native and black Americans have felt the sting and suffering of the sins against their forefathers, so white Americans have enjoyed the benefits of the wrongs that were done to these people.

White Americans should also repent of acts of oppression. These acts may include sins of omission as well as commission. The sins of apathy and pride are as devastating as stereotyping and injustice. To whom does one confess? It is possible to be so general in repentance that confession loses its significance. It's also possible to confess to the wrong person. When Judas repented he went to the high priest rather than to Christ (Matthew 27:3-4). We need to repent with wisdom and articulation.

RECONCILING

Churches can decide how and to whom they will repent. If reconciliation is to be effective, it will take place at a variety of levels—across denominational lines and within individual churches. But the most effective reconciliation is at the local level. The best context for reconciliation is within a region, city, or neighborhood where personal interchange can take place.

Resolution cannot be accomplished simply through a statement, pronouncement, or speech. It comes through restitution (if appropriate) and dialog. Reconciliation should involve not only leadership but also church members talking on a spiritual and social level. Establishing a common prayer emphasis between peoples is a good way to begin. Providing opportunities to build familiarity with one another is imperative.

In the *Christianity Today* survey referred to earlier, the most often repeated response to the question, "What must be done for race relations to be improved?" was, "Let's get to know each other."[8] Reconciliation may be easier for residents in some geographic areas than others, but it is never easy to admit sin, seek forgiveness, and take the necessary steps toward reconciliation.

RECOGNIZING

"When all has been said and done, more has been said than done," someone once said. After repenting and reconciling must come action, not just more words. In an interview with Charles H. King, founder of the Urban Crisis Center in Atlanta, the interviewer commented, "Most Christian people when speaking about love for their own families, are talking about loving action; but when it comes to racism, love becomes philosophical or a matter of prayer.[9]

There are two phases of recognizing multiracial and multiethnic people and churches. First, we must recognize their legitimacy. If people and churches are regarded as inferior because of their facilities, leadership training, or style of worship, the basis for racial harmony is destroyed. Most people of color, including clergy, have not had the same educational opportunities as the white majority. Many minority pastors are forced to be bivocational for economic reasons.

Another way to recognize racial and ethnic groups is to learn about their differences and celebrate their cultural contributions. Some churches have a black or Hispanic history month, where speakers come to talk about their history, special traditions, and celebrations. This could be done to acquaint people with Native Americans, Asian-Americans, and other cultures. One group designed a cultural calendar in which ethnic events, as well as local and national events, were featured. Some denominations, such as the Southern Baptist Convention, have a Race Relations Sunday each year. The focus may be on a racial problem in the community or an event in the history of a different culture. After recognizing other racial and cultural groups, the next step toward racial harmony is reciprocation.

RECIPROCATING

Racial harmony, if it becomes a reality, involves reciprocal relationships. Effective growing relationships involve give and take. An article titled "The Mirror of God" highlights this essential element:

> Without a sense of equal need and equal contribution among Christians, there can be no equal concern. All the parts must see themselves as God intended: that they be both givers and receivers, needed and needy. When we begin to see ourselves as equally needed parts of the mir-

ror that reflects our Creator, we will move closer to complete unity and will reflect more clearly the image of Christ to the world, in all his glory, power and love.[10]

In the process of attaining unity, it is extremely important that white congregations listen to the insights of the minority and accept their feelings. That means that the white majority does not expect leadership in combined efforts to be white. In a truly reciprocal relationship, people of color must be represented in visible ways.

Where possible, churches can begin reciprocating by linking up with a church of a different racial make-up. A "sister church" can be established within a community or within a metropolitan area. For example, an inner-city church might link up with a suburban church. One of the easiest ways to begin the process is to have a pulpit exchange or a choir exchange between churches. Prior to or following one of these Sunday exchanges, members of one congregation could invite members from the other congregation into their homes for a meal.

Other ways of reciprocating might be to cosponsor a food shelf, retreat, leadership seminar, or youth program. It is surprising how many creative possibilities can emerge when ideas and concerns are shared.

RESOURCING

Before entering into joint projects, it is important to discover what has already been done and what is being done in the community to meet needs and combat racism and injustice. Networking with existing church ministries and community agencies will enlarge possibilities.

One of the biggest problems that many ethnic churches face is a lack of resources. The needs are great, and there is always a shortage of funds and personnel to support their ministries. For example, a participating church can assist an ethnic church in day-care or tutoring.

Scholarship funds allow minority children to go to camps and retreats. They also help provide spiritual, mental, physical, and social growth for young people. Scholarships may also be used to provide funds for potential leaders. Theological education is beyond the reach of many minority students today because of insufficient financial aid. Congregations could work together to sponsor minority students, particularly those of races and cultures different from their own. Money could also be designated through church mission programs to aid minority churches.

Will any of these activities end racism in the church? No. Will synergistic efforts make a difference in race relations in the United States? Yes. Black theologian James Earl Massey supports the need for majority churches to work together with racial and ethnic churches. "Given the trend of exclusiveness within society and church, our task will not be easy or readily achievable. But it can be faithful, rightly inspired, and reasonably informed to make a difference with the help of God."[11]

Instead of mimicking society's prejudices, Christians have the opportunity to create a climate where love and understanding prevail over prejudice and racism.

> It was an ancient rabbi who asked his students how they could tell when night had ended and the day was on its way back.
> "Could it be when you see an animal in the distance and can tell whether it is a sheep or a dog?"
> "No," answered the rabbi.

"Could it be when you look at a tree in the distance and can tell whether it is a fig tree or a peach tree?"

"No," answered the rabbi.

"Well then, when is it?" the students demanded.

"It is when you look at the face of any woman or man and see that she or he is your brother or sister. Because if you cannot do this then no matter what time it is, it is still night."[12]

As our relationships between our children and their spouses have grown stronger, we've found a new freedom to express ourselves more honestly. During a recent visit, Martha asked Anita something she'd wanted to know for a long time. "Mom, were you more concerned with my background or my skin color when Mark and I wanted to be married?"

Anita knew she had to be truthful. Selecting her words with care, she answered, "Martha, I'm ashamed to admit this, but it was only your skin color that bothered me."

Martha was surprised. "I always thought it was my background," she said.

Their discussion could never have taken place during the first few years of their acquaintance, as Martha almost never initiated a conversation. Frightened and shy of her northern, educated in-laws, she politely answered our questions with one or two words. Today Martha is a college student and a wife and mother of two active children. Her newfound confidence has given her courage to ask questions that have bothered her for many years.

As a family we've come a long way, and we continue to appreciate each other more and more. We can honestly say that we are proud of our children and their choices of lifetime marriage partners. As part of an interracial family we will continue to speak out against racism and encourage other families who struggle with this issue. When our children crossed racial boundaries to marry, they challenged society, as have others before them. Their offspring will continue to challenge society, for not everyone will be willing to accept the choices they've made. However, our family is only a small part of this growing phenomenon.

Perhaps this book has brought you one step closer to seeing race relations clearly, even while society sees only the night. The apostle Paul stated the Christian viewpoint when he said, "From now on we regard no one from a worldly point of view" (2 Corinthians 5:16). As each of us begins to see people from God's viewpoint, we will learn not to judge them by the color of their skin but by the clarity of our vision.

Notes

1. Bobby Gross, "Racism with a Smile," *His* (February 1985): 2.
2. Kyle Haselden, *Mandate for White Christians* (Richmond: John Knox, 1966), p. 48.
3. David Gelman with Karen Breilsford and Mark Miller, "Black and White in America," *Newsweek* (March 7, 1988): 18-23.
4. Amy Kuebelbeck, "Separation of Church," *Seattle Times*, September 2, 1990, sec. A.
5. Randall L. Frame, "Race and the Church: A Progress Report," *Christianity Today* (March 4, 1988): 16-17.
6. Paul B. Henry, in *The Chicago Declaration*, ed. Ronald J. Sider (Carol Stream, Ill.: Creation House, 1974), p. 138.
7. Michael Verchot, "Taking the Steps Toward Racial Injustice," *Sojourners*, A Study Guide on White Racism (1988): 107.
8. Frame, "Race and the Church: A Progress Report," pp. 16-17.
9. "White People Must Change—An Interview with Charles King," *Sojourners* (May 1981): 21.
10. Stanley K. Inouye, "The Mirror of God," *Christianity Today* (March 3, 1989): 28.
11. James Earl Massey, "Coloring of America," *Christianity Today* (January 17, 1986): 1.
12. Quoted in Dick Brogan, comp., *Not Our Kind of Folks?* (Nashville: Broadman, 1976), 65. From Joseph T. Nolan, ed., *Good Newsletter* 4, issue 4 (April 1977): 145.

Glossary

Acculturation—the process by which an individual born into one culture and moving to another becomes similar as far as humanly possible in thought patterns, language, idealism, and so on to the people of the adopted culture

Amalgamation—the biological union of peoples and the creation of new racial stock

Assimilation—absorption into the cultural tradition of a population or group by changing cultural patterning and personal attitudes

Caste—a system of rigid social stratification characterized by hereditary status, endogamy, and social barriers sanctioned by custom, law, or religion

Culture—the sum total of ways of living learned by a group of human beings and transmitted from one generation to another

Enculturation—the process by which a person learns or acquires acceptance in his or her own culture

Endogamy—marriage within a specific group as required by custom or law

Ethnic—a member of a minority group who retains the customs, language, or social views of his or her group

Ethnicity—a collectivity within a larger society having common ancestry, memories of a shared historical past, and a cultural focus

Ethnocentric—characterized by or based on the attitude that one's own group is superior; tendency to judge other groups in terms of his or her standards

Exogamy—marriage outside of a specific group as required by custom or law

Genotype—the sum total of genes transmitted from parent to offspring

Hegemony—preponderant influence or authority of one nation or group of people over others

Hypergamy—marriage of males of the dominant group to females of the subordinate group

Hypogamy—marriage of males of a lower caste to females of a higher caste

In-marriage—marriage within the group, for example, between two blacks

Interracial marriage—any two racial combinations that enter into a culturally sanctioned marriage

Marginal person—someone living between two cultures without feeling identity with either group

Miscegenation—racial intermixture through marriage, usually referring to the marriage of a white to someone of another race

Mongrel—a person of mixed racial stock, usually used derogatorily

Monogenesis—origin of diverse individuals by descent from a single ancestral individual

Mulatto—a person having one black and one white parent

Out-marriage—marriage with someone of a different racial or ethnic group

Passing—a successful assumption of white status by a person who knows he or she has black ancestry

Phenotype—the outward appearance of a person including hair, nose, lips, but particularly skin color, resulting from the interaction between genotype and environment

Polygenesis—origin of diverse individuals by descent from more than one ancestral source

Race—a grouping of people generally considered physically distinct in some way

Interracial Organizations

CALIFORNIA

Alameda
    Claudia's Caravan (catalog, multicultural materials)
    P.O. Box 1582
    Alameda, CA 94501
    415-521-7871

Gardena
    A Place for Us
    P.O. Box 357
    Gardena, CA 90247
    213-779-1717

Los Angeles
    Multi-Racial Americans of Southern California
    12228 Venice Boulevard, 452
    Los Angeles, CA 90066
    213-856-1535

San Diego
    Image
    3824 Adams Avenue
    San Diego, CA 92116
    619-584-4250

San Francisco
  Association of Multi-Ethnic Americans
      (national organization)
  1060 Tennessee Street
  San Francisco, CA 94107
  415-548-9300

  I-Pride
  1060 Tennessee Street
  San Francisco, CA 94107
  415-548-9300

  Parents' Place (workshops)
  San Francisco, CA
  415-563-1041

COLORADO

  Multi-Racial Families of Colorado
  P.O. Box 20524
  Denver, CO 80220
  303-690-9032

DISTRICT OF COLUMBIA

  Interracial Family Circle
  P.O. Box 53290
  Washington, DC 20001
  301-772-7718

GEORGIA

Atlanta
  Interracial Family Alliance
  P.O. Box 20290
  Atlanta, GA 30325
  404-696-8113

Augusta
Interracial Family Alliance
P.O. Box 9117
Augusta, GA 30906
404-793-8547

ILLINOIS

Biracial Family Network
P.O. Box 489
Chicago, IL 60653
312-288-3644

MAINE

Intercultural Press, Inc.
P.O. Box 700
Yarmouth, ME 04096
207-896-5168

MASSACHUSETTS

Amherst
Biracial Group
953 S.E. Street
Amherst, MA 02002
413-256-0037

Boston
MultiRacial Family Group Network
of Cultural Sharing, Inc.
P.O. Box 554
Boston, MA 02258
617-332-6241

MINNESOTA

Duluth
  Duluth-Superior Interracial Group
  12 E. 4th Street
  Duluth, MN 55805
  218-722-1383

Minneapolis
  Inter-Race (consultants, networking)
  c/o Vivian Jenkins Nelsen
  600 21st Avenue S.
  Minneapolis, MN 55454
  612-339-0820

  Interracial Family Workshops
  Sponsored by Early Childhood Family Education
  Minneapolis Public Schools
  Attention: Ann Freeman
  Lehmann Center, Room 102
  1006 West Lake Street
  Minneapolis, MN 55408
  612-627-2927

  Ours, Inc.
  Suite 203
  3307 Highway North
  Minneapolis, MN 55422

MISSOURI

  Interracial Family Unity Network
  P.O. Box 6754
  Jefferson City, MO 65102
  314-634-2961

NEBRASKA

Lincoln
Lincoln Interracial Network of Citizens
5408 La Salle Street
Lincoln, NE 68512

Omaha
Parents of Interracial Children
115 S. 46th Street
Omaha, NE 68124
402-553-6000

NEW JERSEY
Interracial Family Alliance
194 Northhampton Drive
Willingboro, NJ 08046
609-835-2471

NEW YORK

Buffalo
Interracial Club of Buffalo
P. O. Box 400—Amherst Branch
Buffalo, NY 14226
716-875-6958

Ithaca
Multicultural Resource Center
96 Abbott Lane
Ithaca, NY 14850
607-277-5536

New York
   Biracial Family Resource Center
   800 Riverside Drive, Suite 56
   New York, NY 10032

   Council of Interracial Books For Children
   1841 Broadway
   New York, NY 10023

Schenectady
   Interrace (magazine)
   P.O. Box 1001
   Schenectady, NY 12301

OHIO

Columbus
   Multi-Racial Families of Central Ohio
   P.O. Box 27447
   Columbus, OH 43227
   614-231-2871

Dayton
   Interracial Family Network of Dayton
   5059 Northwest Drive
   Dayton, OH 45414
   513-890-2030

OREGON

Eugene
   Honor Our New Ethnic Youth (H.O.N.E.Y.)
   454 Willamette Avenue, 213
   Eugene, OR 97401
   503-342-3908

Portland
  Interracial Family Network
  P.O. Box 12505
  Portland, OR 97212
  503-282-0612

  People of Every Stripe (catalog,
    multicultural materials)
  P.O. Box 12505
  Portland, OR 97212
  503-282-0612

PENNSYLVANIA

Philadelphia
  Rainbow Circle
  c/o First Baptist Church
  17th and Sansom Street
  Philadelphia, PA 19103

Pittsburgh
  Interracial Families, Inc.
  5450 Friendship Avenue
  Pittsburgh, PA 15232
  412-362-0221

TEXAS

Dallas
  Interracial Partners
  P.O. Box 870803
  Dallas, TX 75252
  214-306-4380

Houston
  Interracial Family Alliance
  P.O. Box 16248
  Houston, TX 77222
  713-454-5018

VIRGINIA

Newport News
  Peninsula Interracial Families
  1096 Palmerton Drive
  Newport News, VA 23602
  804-886-0535

Norfolk
  Interracial Connection
  P.O. Box 7055
  Norfolk, VA 23509
  804-622-9260

WASHINGTON

  Interracial Network
  P.O. Box 344
  Auburn, WA 98071
  206-329-5242

ARMED FORCES

  Multicultural Family Support Group
  4664 W. Rechord Avenue
  Fort Ritchie, MD 21719
  301-241-4462

Selected Bibliography

Allen, James Paul, and Eugene James Turner. *We the People: An Atlas of Ethnic Diversity*. New York: Macmillan, 1988.

Allport, Gordon W. *The Nature of Prejudice*. New York: Doubleday, 1954.

Baum, Gregory, and John Coleman, eds. *The Church and Racism*. New York: Seabury, 1982.

Bode, Janet. *Different Worlds*. New York: Franklin Watts, 1989.

Brogan, Dick, comp. *Not Our Kind of Folks?* Nashville: Broadman, 1978.

Bruno, Leone. *Racism*. St. Paul, Minn.: Greenhaven, 1986.

Buswell, J. Oliver, III. *Slavery, Segregation and Scripture*. Grand Rapids: Eerdmans, 1964.

Crester, Gary A., and Joseph J. Leon, eds. "Intermarriage in the United States." *Marriage and Family Review* 5, no. 1 (1982).

Davies, Alan. *Infected Christianity*. Montreal: McGill-Queens U., 1988.

Dittes, James E. *Bias and the Pious*. Minneapolis: Augsburg, 1973.

Gay, Kathlyn. *The Rainbow Effect*. New York: Franklin Watts, 1987.

164   *Mixed Messages*

Gordon, Albert I. *Intermarriage—Interfaith, Interracial, Interethnic.* Boston: Beacon, 1964.

Haselden, Kyle. *Mandate for White Christians.* Richmond, Va.: Knox, 1966.

————. *The Racial Problem in Christian Perspective.* New York: Harper, 1959.

Jordan, Winthrop. *White Over Black.* Chapel Hill, N.C.: U. of North Carolina, 1968.

Katz, Phyllis, ed. *Towards the Elimination of Racism.* New York: Perganon, 1976.

Klimek, David. *Beneath Mate Selection and Marriage: The Unconscious Motives in Human Pairing.* New York: Van Norstrand Reinhold, 1979.

Larsson, Clotye M., ed. *Marriage Across the Color Line.* Chicago: Johnson, 1965.

Maston, T. B. *Segregation and Desegregation.* New York: Macmillan, 1959.

Montague, Ashley. *Man's Most Dangerous Myth: The Fallacy of Race.* New York: Oxford U., 1974.

Myrdal, Gunnar. *An American Dilemma.* New York: Harper & Row, 1962.

Osseo-Asare, Francislee. *A New Land to Live In.* Downers Grove, Ill.: InterVarsity, 1977.

Pannell, William E. *My Friend the Enemy.* Waco, Tex.: Word, 1968.

Pascoe, Elaine. *Racial Prejudice.* New York: Franklin Watts, 1985.

Perkins, John. *With Justice for All.* Ventura, Calif.: Gospel Light, 1982.

Porterfield, Ernest. *Black and White Mixed Marriages.* Chicago: Nelson-Hall, 1978.

Salley, Columbus, and Ronald Behm. *What Color Is Your God?* Secaucus, N.J.: Citadel, 1988.

Shackford, Kate, ed. "Children of Interracial Families." *Interracial Books for Children Bulletin* 15, no. 6:4-15.

Sider, Ronald J., ed. *The Chicago Declaration*. Carol Stream, Ill.: Creation House, 1974.

Spickard, Paul R. *Mixed Blood*. Madison, Wis.: U. of Wisconsin, 1989.

Stuart, Irving R., and Lawrence E. Abt, eds. *Interracial Marriage: Expectations and Realities*. New York: Grossman, 1973.

Tarplee, Cornelius C. *Racial Prejudice*. Greenwich, Conn.: Seabury, 1962.

Washington, Joseph R., Jr. *Marriage in Black and White*. Boston: Beacon, 1971.

White, Steve, and Ruth. *Free Indeed: The Autobiography of an Interracial Couple*. Gardena, Calif.: A Place for Us, 1989.

Williamson, Joel. *New People: Miscegenation and Mulattoes in the United States*. New York: New York U., 1980.